GW00657468

MARRIAGE CARE COOK BOOK

THE TWELVE DAYS OF CHRISTMAS

PRYOR PUBLICATIONS
WHITSTABLE AND WALSALL

PRYOR PUBLICATIONS
WHITSTABLE AND WALSALL

Specialist in Facsimile Reproductions

MEMBER OF
INDEPENDENT PUBLISHERS GUILD

75 Dargate Road, Yorkletts, Whitstable,
Kent CT5 3AE, England.
Tel. & Fax: (01227) 274655
Email: alan@pryor-publish.clara.net
http://home.clara.net/pryor-publish
Kent Exporter of the Year Awards Winner 1998

1998
Compiled by Virginia Constable Maxwell
Illustrated by Michael Frith

ISBN 0 946014 71 X

A CIP Record for this book is available from the British Library

Marriage Care,
Clitherow House, 1 Blythe Mews,
Blythe Road, London, W14 0NW.
Tel: 0171 371 1341 Fax: 0171 371 4921
E-mail: Marriagecare@btinternet.com
Registered Charity No. 218159

All rights reserved. No part of this publication may be
reproduced, stored in a retrieval system, or transmitted,
in any form or by any means, electronic, mechanical,
photocopying, recording or otherwise, without
the prior permission of the copyright owner.

Printed by
Hillman Printers
(Frome) Ltd.
Handlemaker Road,
Marston Trading Estate,
Frome, Somerset BA11 4RW.
Tel: 01373 473526 Fax: 01373 451852

August, 1998

I wish to express my thanks to all our friends and supporters who have contributed recipes, many of which were entirely unknown to me and delicious beyond words. I am particularly grateful to Alan Pryor, our publisher, who so expertly guided us to completion.

Vanessa Cumberledge, of Books for Cooks, was especially helpful and encouraging at the outset of this project.

I would especially like to thank Mary Corbett, Chief Executive of Marriage Care, who allowed me the time so necessary to compile these recipes; to Brenda Gleave, our Public Relations Manager, without whose expertise we would never have reached a final draft, and both Helen Davies, Business Manager and Angela Dunlea, our Administrative Secretary, whose efforts enabled us to meet our deadline.

Appletree Press, Ltd. in Belfast permitted us, with great generosity, to use the graces to head each chapter.

The Grenadier Guards not only provided us with two outstanding recipes, but also took the time and trouble to give us an incomparable portrait of 'Twelve Drummers Drumming'!

Without doubt, the most generous contribution came from Michael Frith, whose cover, which I have dubbed minimalist chic, and whose motifs which encapsulate each chapter heading with three, perhaps four, inspired strokes, were more than we could ever have expected.

We hope that we can rely on your good will to buy a copy of this book and thank you for your support.

Virginia Constable Maxwell

Virginia Constable Maxwell,
Director of Fund Raising,
Marriage Care.

3

Michael Frith

Michael Frith is one of those rare painters who can make something out of nothing. He reveals the beauty in what most of us take for granted and therefore never really see.

He does this in his food illustrations for the '*Sunday Times*'. In a few seemingly casual washes and flicks of the brush he brings a humble turnip, fish or ricotta cheese to thrilling life.

He is a master of portraiture too, using the transparency and fluidity of watercolour to create a vivid likeness and suggest the personality behind it. In some of his portraits he achieves what most watercolourists think impossible- a coherent image on a phenomenally large scale. The face of his Robert Maxwell (in the National Portrait Gallery) is no less than five feet high. The size helps evoke the intimidating physical presence the man had in life, but his devious charm is conveyed just as convincingly.

In equally extraordinary seascapes Frith tests the limits of his notoriously difficult medium. Some of these watercolours are so big that he had to paint them on the floor, using a map as well as brushes and waiting for up to a day for each expansive wash to dry. But their size is not the most impressive thing about Frith's seascapes. They are extraordinarily beautiful images which give tantalising glimpses of the way in which essentially abstract effects can be made to create fragile, evanescent illusions of reality.

In Frith's paintings, each confident spontaneous mark looks as though it came about of its own accord. But what seems to have come together effortlessly is as much the artful product of natural talent, concentrated practice and rich experience as a brilliant display of technique and sensibility by a virtuoso pianist. Michael Frith is quite simply one of the finest watercolourists working anywhere today.

Frank Whitford
Art historian & critic

Marriage Care

Marriage Care is a national charity which carries both the history and experience of more than fifty years in the support of marriage. At its heart is relationship counselling, with other complementary services radiating from it.

As an organisation, love is our guiding principle. Not simply romantic love but a love which describes the nature of commitment to a relationship for life. Marriage Care has a vision of marriage which is secure, dynamic and potentially creative. Its purpose is to help people prepare for, achieve and sustain successful marriages and to support them should their marriages break down.

With seventy centres located in and around major towns throughout England and Wales, Marriage Care can lay claim to a national network of relationship counsellors. All Marriage Care's counsellors are volunteers who are trained to a standard accredited by the College of Ripon & York St John, University of Leeds. Consequently, the form of counselling which they practise combines both professional skills and distinctive personal qualities. A key benefit to clients is a service without charge, although those with the financial means are invited to make a donation.

Drawing on its particular expertise, Marriage Care also designs and manages marriage preparation courses. Operating from a parish base, multi-disciplinary teams work in, and for, the local community. They encourage couples to explore, test and in some cases, renew their commitment to marriage.

'The Twelve Days of Christmas' is our unique way of celebrating marriage at what is traditionally regarded as a family time. What better carol to adopt for a first festive offering from Marriage Care than words which embrace the dual theme of love and giving! We hope that you will sample and enjoy these recipes which will excite both appetite and imagination.

The Twelve Days of Christmas

'The Twelve Days of Christmas' is found in different forms in broadsides from the fifteenth century and derives from a traditional Twelfth Night forfeits game in which each person was required to recite a list of objects named by the previous player and add one more. The tune - one of many - realised its modern standard form only in 1909, with the inspired addition of the phrase to which '5 gold rings' is sung. (Music Frederic Austin Version: Copyright Novello & Co Ltd.)

For every fifteenth-century carol that appears in more than one manuscript, it is represented in more than one form. 'The Twelve Days of Christmas' is no exception, as demonstrated by the alternative traditional English rhyme below.

> *'4th day - four canary birds*
> *5th day - five gold rings*
> *6th day - geese a laying*
> *7th day - swans a swimming*
> *8th day - deers a running*
> *9th day - lads a leaping*
> *10th day - ladies skipping*
> *11th day - bears a baiting*
> *12th day - parsons preaching'*

Carols are songs with a religious impulse that are simple, hilarious, popular, and modern. They are generally spontaneous and direct in expression, and their simplicity of form causes them sometimes to ramble like a ballad. The word 'carol' has a dancing origin, and once meant to dance in a ring. The carol, in fact, by forsaking the timeless contemplative melodies of the Church, began the era of modern music, which has throughout been based upon the dance.

The typical carol gives voice to the common emotions of healthy people in language that can be understood and music that can be shared by all. It dances because it is so Christian, echoing St. Paul's conception of the fruits of the spirit in its challenge to be merry - 'Love and joy come to you...'

Contents

VIII - Maids a Milking - Grace
Oeufs Florentines, Cheese and Ham Soufflé, Cheese and Watercress Flan, Boot Pie, Dolcelatte and Mascarpone Sauce, Cheese Cake.

IX - Ladies Dancing - Grace
Courgette and Dill Soup, Spinach Tart, Curried Chicken Casserole, Mick's Goulash, Grilled Red Mullet, Creamed Courgettes, Apricot and Hazelnut Meringue, Quick Almond Bavaroise, Chocolate Nests, Fudge Drops.

X- Lords a Leaping - Grace
Bruges Eggs, Watercress Soup, Grilled Aubergine Pesto, Lamb Casserole, Jugged Hare/Rabbit, Chocolate Delight, Dark Banana Surprise.

XI - Pipers Piping - Grace
Birchan Avocados, Hungarian Meatball Soup, Boned Chicken Stuffed with Bulgar Wheat, Apricots and Pine Nuts, Shamrock Chicken, Baked Ham with Madeira and Raisin Sauce, Mascarenhas Goan Trifle, Baked Stuffed Apples, Pumpkin Walnut Pie.

XII - Drummers Drumming - Grace
Thick Vegetable Soup, Lamb Braised in Beaujolais, Apostles' Casserole, Turkey Upholland, Raised Pie, Noisettes of Lamb 'Twelve Drummers Drumming', Leek and Potato Gratin, 'Instant on the Lips, Lifetime on the Hips' Cheesecake, Fresh Redcurrant Flan, Christmas Pudding.

I

On the First day of Christmas
My true love sent to me,
A Partridge in a Pear Tree.

'Starting the Day
This is the day the Lord has made-
Give thanks for toast and marmalade.'

Mushroom and Coriander Salad

Serves 4

Ms Brenda Gleave

Ingredients

1lb small/button mushrooms
¼ pint dry white wine
1 teaspoon coriander seeds (crushed)
dressing
1 clove garlic
1 teaspoon salt
1 tablespoon dry vinegar
½ teaspoon brown sugar
1 teaspoon French mustard
¼ pint olive oil
1 tablespoon chopped parsley
1 small onion (very finely chopped)
6 black olives (stoned and finely chopped)
black pepper (freshly milled)

Method
Clean mushrooms. Separate stalks from caps and put into a pan with wine and coriander. Bring to simmering point and simmer until all the wine has evaporated. (Shake the pan, so that mushrooms are evenly cooked.)

To prepare dressing
Place garlic, salt, sugar, mustard and wine vinegar in a screwtop jar and leave for a few minutes until salt and sugar have dissolved. Add olive oil and shake jar. Next, add onion, parsley, olives and pepper. Transfer mushrooms to a serving bowl. Pour dressing over them whilst they are still warm. Leave to cool, then chill in fridge. Serve with crusty bread.

Spinach Roll

Serves 4

Mrs Marinos Costeletos

Ingredients

3lbs of fresh spinach or
3 pkgs of frozen chopped spinach
6 tablespoons butter
salt
pepper
nutmeg
Parmesan cheese
4 eggs (separated)

Method
Cook spinach. Drain, chop coarsely, if fresh. Season with butter, salt, pepper and nutmeg.
Add egg yolks one at a time.
Beat whites until softly mounted. Fold into spinach mixture.

Pour into a pan 11" x 15½" lined with waxed paper that has been buttered and sprinkled with bread crumbs.

Sprinkle with grated Parmesan cheese and bake at 350F for 12-16 minutes. Cover with buttered foil and invert. Fill with softly scrambled eggs. Roll. Serve at once.

Eggs Baked in Tomatoes

Serves 4

Mrs Theresa Pride

Ingredients

4 large firm tomatoes (ideally French ones)
4 slices of bread
4 egg yolks
4 teaspoons double cream
1 tablespoon grated Parmesan cheese
2 teaspoons tomato purée
1 clove garlic

Method
Wash and dry tomatoes.
Slice off tops with sharp knife.
Scoop out pulp.

Sprinkle inside with salt and pressed or finely chopped garlic.
Turn tomatoes upside down to drain for 30 minutes.
Break egg and place yolk into the tomato shell.
Season with salt and pepper.
Blend tomato purée with the cream and spoon over the eggs.
Sprinkle each tomato with grated Parmesan cheese. Put tomatoes in oven proof dish. Bake near top of oven 350F/gas mark 4/ 180C for 15-20 minutes or until the eggs have just set. Cut the bread into circles with scone/pastry cutter. Heat 1 oz butter and 2 teaspoons of olive oil in frying pan. Fry the bread until crisp and golden on both sides. Serve one tomato on each round of bread.

Partridge and Chestnut Stew

Serves 4

Mrs Andrew Howden

Ingredients

2 brace partridge (prepared)
8 oz chestnuts
8 oz onions
1 oz butter
1 level tablespoon flour
1 pint hot chicken stock
1 tablespoon redcurrant jelly
2 - 3 rinds of large oranges
juice of one orange
1 teaspoon wine vinegar
1 bay leaf
salt and pepper
chopped parsley

Method
Set oven to 180C.

Peel onions and fry partridge in butter. Place in casserole. Fry the onions. Add the flour to butter and make a roux. Gradually add stock, redcurrant jelly, orange juice, rind and vinegar. Whisk this and pour into casserole, add the chestnuts and cook for an hour. Strain the cooking liquid and reduce for five minutes.

Partridge, Pear and Rosemary

Serves 6

Mrs James Corbett

Ingredients

3 brace partridge
8 oz softened butter
1 clove garlic
½ teaspoon ground rosemary
1 teaspoon salt and pepper
6 bacon rashers
2 sliced onions
sprigs of rosemary
1 teaspoon flour
6 firm but ripe pears

¾ pint full bodied Spanish red wine
2 cloves
1 bay leaf

Method
Pre-heat the oven to gas mark 9.

Mix the butter, garlic, salt, pepper and rosemary into a rough paste. Smear this all over and inside the fowl. Cover the breasts with the rashers and place on a sliced onion and rosemary sprigs in a roasting tin. After 15 minutes' oven time reduce the heat to gas mark 7 and cook for a further 15 - 20 minutes.

Meanwhile, peel the pears and arrange them in a heavy saucepan. Pour the wine, cloves, rosemary and bay leaf mixture over the pears, bring to the boil, turn down the heat, cover and allow to poach for approx 30 minutes. Remove pears and keep warm when cooked.

Remove the birds from the roasting tin. Keep warm. Pour away excess fat and remove the rosemary. Sprinkle in the flour, let this brown and add, gradually, half the wine in which the pears were cooked. Bring to the boil, reduce the heat and simmer for 2 minutes. Strain into warm sauceboat.

Arrange the partridge and pears together with rosemary sprigs on a warm serving dish.

(The remaining strained wine can be further reduced with the addition of 2 oz castor sugar made into a delicious syrup which can be reserved for serving with ice cream).

Pheasant with Port and Cointreau

Serves 4

Mr Michael Frith

Ingredients

A brace of pheasant
2 onions (peeled and sliced)
mixed herbs
salt and pepper
orange rind
orange juice (1 glass)

Port (1 glass)
1 tablespoon of Cointreau
vegetable - carrots, leeks or mushrooms
bouquet garni
bay leaves

Method
Portion pheasants into four. Sauté onions gently in olive oil. Remove them from pan and fry garlic and mixed herbs in pan. Seal the pheasant portions one by one with the garlic and herbs. Put aside in large casserole dish and meanwhile grate orange rind over pheasant portions. Add all other ingredients. Slam in the oven for about 1½ hours at 160C.

Pheasant with Cream and Apples

Serves 2

Mr David Wagg

Ingredients

1 young pheasant
1 oz butter
1 tablespoon oil
½ onion chopped
3 medium Cox's apples
6 oz dry cider
5 oz double cream
salt and pepper

Method
Heat butter and oil together in casserole.
Season pheasant with salt and pepper.
Brown in hot fat, turning over. Add onion and cook till transparent.
Meanwhile quarter, core and peel apples. Slice them and place in casserole. Add cider. Turn bird on side and cook in casserole over a very low heat for about an hour. Half way through, turn bird on other side.

Remove pheasant and heat the liquid till most has evaporated, leaving the apples. Stir in cream and season. Pour sauce over pheasant.

Broccoli-Apple Purée

Serves 2

Mrs Marinos Costeletos

Ingredients

1lb broccoli florets (coarsely chopped)
2 apples (peeled and diced)
2 shallots (chopped)
2 oz butter
8 oz chicken stock
2 oz double cream

Method
Sauté shallots, apples and broccoli in 1oz butter. Add stock and cover. Simmer for 5 minutes covered. Remove cover and continue to cook gently until almost all the liquid has evaporated.

Purée in food-processor leaving the texture coarse. Blend in 1oz soft butter and 2oz double cream.
Taste for seasoning and adjust with salt, pepper and freshly grated nutmeg. Re-warm gently.

Apples and Pears

Serves 2

Ms Dianne Farris

Ingredients

2 cooking apples
2 firm pears
butter
dates
brown sugar
sherry

Method
Peel and core fruit and cut into chunks. Put in shallow oven-proof dish. Mix in brown sugar to taste and some chopped dates. Moisten a little with sherry and dot with a little butter. Bake at top of hot oven.

Pears in Red Wine

Serves 6

Mrs Peter Constable Maxwell

Ingredients

6 large hard pears
1 pint red wine
4oz sugar
2 cinnamon sticks
1 vanilla pod
1 dessertspoon arrowroot
¾ pint whipped cream

Method
Preheat oven to 250F -130C.

Peel pears and place in large casserole. Separately boil red wine, sugar and cinnamon. Add vanilla pod and pour over pears. Cover and bake for 3 hours, turning half time. Pour liquid into saucepan and add small amount of arrowroot blended with cold water. Boil, stirring constantly, until mixture has slightly thickened.

Cool and pour over pears. Serve with whipped cream. A festive and colourful pudding over Christmas!

American Brownies

Makes 12

Mrs Peter Brown

Ingredients

4oz butter
2oz plain chocolate (melted)
2 eggs (beaten)
2oz plain flour (sifted)
8oz brown sugar
1 teaspoon baking powder
¼ teaspoon salt
4oz nuts (either pecans, almonds, walnuts, brazils or all four)

Method
Mix all dry ingredients in a bowl, then add the eggs, the melted butter and chocolate. Stir in the broken up nuts and spread in a prepared Swiss roll tin. Cook at 180C for 30 minutes and cut while still warm.

These brownies do not have the consistency of cake. They are moist and chewy, squidgy and nutty chocolate mouthfuls that you can bite into and not worry about crumbs. Don't overcook them - they are supposed to be fairly dense in the middle. Enjoy.

Apricot, Prune and Walnut Mincemeat

The Duchess of Norfolk

Ingredients

4oz currants
4oz no-soak prunes (chopped)
4oz sultanas
4oz no-soak apricots (chopped)
2oz cut mixed peel
1 large cooking apple (peeled and cored)
2oz walnut pieces
4oz shredded suet
8oz Demerara sugar
1 teaspoon mixed spice
¼ pint brandy or rum

Method

Chop finely the dried fruit, apples and nuts. Place in a large bowl (non-metal). Add the suet, spices, sugar and mix in enough spirits to give a moist mixture.

Cover and leave to stand for 2 days, stirring every so often. Mix well again and put into clean jars, pressing well down. Cover with a layer of cling film and then screw the jar lid on tightly.

Allow to mature for 2 weeks before using.

This is a alternative to Traditional Christmas Mincemeat.

II

On the Second day of Christmas
My true love sent to me;
Two Turtle Doves ,
and a Partridge in a Pear Tree

'It is very nice to think
The world is full of meat and drink
With little children saying Grace
In every Christian kind of place'

19th Century, Robert Louis Stevenson

Very Strong Chicken Broth

Serves 4

Mrs Gregory Stainow

Ingredients

1 good fat hen
1 carrot
1 stick celery (chopped)
1 unpeeled onion (chopped)
bouquet garni of 1 bayleaf, 4 parsley stalks, sprig of rosemary and thyme
salt and freshly ground pepper

Method
Put the bird in a large, heavy saucepan with the vegetables. Cover with water. Bring slowly to the boil and simmer for 3 - 4 hours. Remove the chicken. Leave the stock overnight to cool, and chill the chicken. Next day, skin the fat from the stock. Return the chicken to the stock and boil uncovered until the liquid is reduced almost by half. Remove the chicken again and allow the stock to cool again. Take out the bouquet garni. Remove any remaining fat from the jellied stock. Heat quantities as required. Season with salt and pepper.

Spiced Prawn Starter

Serves 6

Mrs John Poncia MBE

Ingredients

2lb very large, peeled cooked prawns
juice of 1 lemon (plus 1 lemon, thinly sliced)
2 - 3 teaspoons fresh lime juice
several leaves fresh coriander
½ teaspoon ground cumin
½ teaspoon paprika
pinch cayenne
3 tablespoons olive oil
1 garlic clove (halved)
salt and pepper
rocket and other sharp green salad leaves
dressing

Method
Put the prawns into a glass dish and sprinkle with lemon juice, coriander leaves, cumin, paprika and cayenne. Season lightly and toss well, then cover with lemon slices. Cover and chill for a few hours.

Rub a frying pan with the cut sides of garlic. Heat the olive oil. Drain the prawns, discarding lemon slices, but keep the juice for later. Add prawns to the pan and sauté for 3 minutes over the high heat, pushing them around the pan to colour evenly. At the last moment, add the lime and lemon juices and let it cook with the prawns.

Arrange the dressed salad on plates and then scatter the prawns on top. Serve with wedges of lemon and Ciabatta bread.

Garlic Mushrooms

Serves 4

Mrs Truda-Anne Lee

Ingredients

1lb field mushrooms
2 cloves garlic
2oz butter

Method
Place mushrooms in shallow individual oven-proof dishes. Add knobs of butter and garlic to taste. Put in hot oven until butter has melted and mushrooms are cooked.
Garnish with parsley and serve straight from oven to table.

Tuscan Bean Soup

Serves 6 - 8

Mrs Nicholas Haydon

Ingredients

2 tablespoons olive oil
1 clove garlic (finely chopped)
1 carrot
1 celery rib (chopped)
2 leeks (chopped)
1 sprig rosemary (finely chopped)
1 dried red chilli pepper (de-seeded and crushed)
1 pound dried white beans (washed, soaked overnight and drained)
1 ham bone
salt and pepper
6 - 8 tablespoons grated Parmesan cheese
1 onion (thinly sliced)

Method
Heat oil in a large heavy bottomed pan and sauté garlic, onion, carrot, celery, leeks, rosemary and chilli pepper until just browned. Add beans, ham bone and 5 pints water, simmer covered, for 2 hours. Season with salt and pepper. Remove ham bone and rub half the beans through a fine sieve (or purée in a blender). Return purée to the soup and heat through. Serve in soup bowls, garnished with cheese and onion.

Baked Peppers

Serves 2

Mr and Mrs Peter Ball

Ingredients

3 red peppers
Greek yoghurt
fromage frais
Parmesan and grated Gruyère
paprika, fresh herbs (optional)

Method
Cut peppers in two, lengthways and remove the seeds. Fill halves with a mixture of yoghurt, fromage frais, some grated Gruyère and a pinch of Parmesan. (You can add chives, or paprika, to vary the flavour). Bake in medium hot oven for approximately 40 minutes.

Braised Venison

Serves 4

Mrs Peter Constable Maxwell

Ingredients

1 joint of venison, marinated overnight in ½ pint red wine, 3 tablespoons olive oil, root vegetables and 6 crushed juniper berries
2 onions
2 sticks celery
2 carrots
bouquet garni
½ pint stock
rind and juice of 1 orange
salt and pepper
1 dessertspoon red currant jelly

Method
Wipe, dry and brown the meat all over in hot oil or fat. Slice the onions, celery and carrots, and fry gently for 5 minutes in the same oil. Place the vegetables in a casserole and put the meat on top. Add bouquet garni, strained marinade, stock and orange peel. Season, cover and braise 2 - 2½ hours at 325F (gas mark 3). Baste occasionally. When cooked, slice and arrange on a heated serving dish. Strain the casserole juices, reduce a little. Add orange juice and redcurrant jelly and thicken with arrowroot.

Spoon some sauce over the meat and serve rest separately.

Port Jello

Serves 4

Mrs Carol Costello

Ingredients

1 packet lemon jello
½ pint water
¾ pint port

Method
Dissolve jello in port and water.
Mix well.

Leave in fridge for several hours in chosen serving dish.
Top with whipped cream and burnt almonds.

Fudgy Fruit Crumble

Serves 2

Miss Elizabeth Constable Maxwell

Ingredients

1 apple
1½ tablespoons sugar
4oz plain flour
2oz margarine
1½oz brown sugar

Method
Heat oven to gas mark 5/190C/375F.
Chop apple. Put into heat-proof dish. Sprinkle with sugar. Rub flour and fat together using tips of fingers. Mix in brown sugar and sprinkle topping over fruit. Place on baking sheet and cook for 15 minutes. Reduce heat to gas mark 3/170C/325F and cook for a further 15 minutes. Allow to cool slightly before serving.

Old Fashioned Apple Pie

Serves 6

Mrs Stephen Wheatcroft

Ingredients

frozen shortcrust pastry

Filling
4 large cooking apples (peeled, cored, sliced)
2 tablespoons water
2oz butter
2 tablespoons caster sugar
3 digestive biscuits (crushed)
2 tablespoons brandy
grated peel of lemon
⅛ pint of double cream
3 egg yolks
freshly grated nutmeg

Method
Pre-heat oven to 350F.
Roll out frozen pastry and place in 8" lightly-greased flan tin. Bake blind until partly cooked.

Gently simmer apples in water till soft. Place in large bowl and whip till smooth. Add butter and caster sugar, followed by biscuit crumbs, lemon peel, brandy and grated nutmeg. Cool. Beat egg yolks together with cream. Add to cooled apple mixture. Pour whole lot into partly cooked flan case and bake in oven for 30 minutes.

III

On the Third day of Christmas,
My true Love gave to me;
Three French Hens,
Two Turtle Doves and
A Partridge in a Pear Tree

'Here a little child I stand,
Heaving up my either hand;
Cold as paddocks though they be,
Here I lift them up to thee,
For a benison to fall,
On our meat and on us all'

17th Century, Robert Robert Herrick

Red Pepper Soup

Serves 4 - 6

Mrs Hora den Dulk

Ingredients

1 tablespoon olive oil
1 large onion (peeled and chopped)
2 cloves garlic (crushed)
3 large red peppers (cored and sliced)
1 medium potato (peeled and diced)
2 tablespoons tomato purée
2 large tomatoes (skinned and chopped)
1¾ pints hot stock
salt and freshly ground black pepper
freshly chopped parsley or chives
2 tablespoons natural yoghurt or single cream

Method
Heat the oil in a heavy-based pan and fry the onions gently until soft. Add the garlic, cook for a few minutes more, then stir in the peppers, potato, tomato purée and tomatoes. Add the hot stock and seasoning, bring to the boil, cover and simmer for 30 minutes. Leave to cool slightly and liquidise.

Re-heat to serve and put a teaspoon of yoghurt or single cream on top of each bowl of soup and add a sprinkling of chopped parsley or chives. Serve with warm bread and butter.

Spring Rolls with Prawn and Bean Sprout Filling

Serves 4

Mrs Marinos Costeletos

Ingredients

2 tablespoons sesame oil
1 tablespoon corn oil
1 tablespoon minced ginger
1 teaspoon minced garlic
2 handfuls bean sprouts
8oz prawns (chopped)
1 tin minced water chestnuts
2 slices smoked ham (minced)
3 - 4 spring onions
1 grated carrot
2 tablespoons soy sauce
2 teaspoons cornstarch mixed with 2 tablespoon water
filo pastry
butter
sesame seeds

Method
Pre-heat oven to 375F.
Stir fry ginger and garlic in the oils for 30 seconds. Add bean sprouts, chopped prawns, chestnuts, minced ham, onions and carrot. Stir fry for about 2 minutes. Add soy sauce and cornstarch mixture and stir till vegetables glaze slightly. Cool. Brush squares of pastry with melted butter. Fill with mixture. Brush rolls with butter and sprinkle with sesame seeds. Place in oven for 10-15 minutes.

Chicken Liver and Sage Ragu

Serves 4

Mrs Virginia Lopalco

This is a delicious sauce made with chicken livers, Panchetta or smoked bacon.

Ingredients

1lb Pasta Reale fresh tagliatelle

Sauce
1 large onion (finely chopped)
7oz Panchetta or smoked bacon (chopped)
14oz chicken livers (cleaned and finely chopped)
2 cloves garlic (finely chopped)
4/5 leaves of fresh sage
pinch of cinnamon
2 tablespoons tomato purée
1 tablespoon butter
1 medium glass of white wine or water
salt and freshly milled black pepper
Parmesan cheese to sprinkle

Method
Fry the onion and garlic in the oil until transparent. Add the chicken livers and sage leaves. Keep stirring for 2/3 minutes then add the tomato purée, cinnamon and white wine (or water). Add salt to taste, cook gently for 20 minutes and at the very last moment add the butter and freshly milled black pepper.

Cook the pasta as directed on the packet and dress with the sauce. Sprinkle with Parmesan cheese.

Chicken in a Lemon Cream and White Wine Sauce

Serves 6

Mrs Kate Chalmers

Ingredients

6 chicken breasts (skinned)
1 large lemon (juice and rind)
3 tablespoons sherry
4 tablespoons white wine
½ pint cream (whipping)
salt and pepper to taste

Method
Melt 2oz butter. Brown chicken breasts approx 5 minutes on each side. Remove from pan. Add the juices, lemon juice and rind, sherry and white wine. Reduce liquid by half. Remove from heat.

Add the cream to reduced liquid in the pan and stir until well blended, add salt, and pepper. Put chicken breasts in oven proof dish. Pour sauce over. Add grated cheese (optional). Cook without a lid for about 30 minutes until the chicken is tender. Moderate temperature 160C/gas mark 5.

Roast Chicken with Apricots

Serves 4-6

Miss Sarah Anderson

Ingredients

4 tablespoons butter
6 tablespoons honey
1 teaspoon rose water
½ teaspoon freshly grated nutmeg
1 teaspoon rose water
½ teaspoon freshly grated nutmeg
1 teaspoon salt
½ teaspoon freshly ground pepper
1 4lb roasting chicken
1lb fresh apricots (pitted and halved)
6 - 8 tablespoons toasted almonds

Method
Combine butter, 4 tablespoons of the honey, rose water, nutmeg, salt and pepper and rub chicken inside and out. Place chicken in a roasting tin and roast in a preheated 425F oven until golden, about 45 minutes. Lower heat to 350F and add apricots and remaining honey to pan juices. Continue roasting for 20 minutes or until tender. Remove chicken to a warm platter, pour pan juices and apricots over chicken, sprinkle with nuts and serve with hot buttered rice.

Harlequin Pasta

Serves 4

Miss Linda Robson

Ingredients

1 red pepper
1 green pepper
2 leeks
6oz button mushrooms
12oz pasta
1 clove garlic
salt and pepper
2 tablespoons oil
4 tablespoons single cream
8oz sweetcorn
fresh basil

Method

Seed and chop peppers and slice leeks and mushrooms. Put the pasta in a large pan of fast boiling water and cook for 10 - 12 minutes until just tender. Drain. Meanwhile, make sauce. Heat oil in frying pan. Add leeks and mushrooms and fry for 2 - 3 minutes. Crush or chop garlic, add to pan along with peppers. Fry for 3 - 4 minutes. Add cream and sweetcorn. Add pasta and stir well. Heat for 2 - 3 minutes. Season and serve garnished with plenty of basil.

PAULINE QUIRKE & LINDA ROBSON

Alomo Productions, A Pearson Television Company for BBC

Caribbean Christmas Cake

Mrs Marinos Costeletos

Ingredients

1lb sultanas
2lbs mixed fruit
8oz stoned raisins
8oz currants
1lb butter
1lb soft brown sugar
10 eggs
1lb plain flour
4oz ground almonds
4oz chopped cherries
1 dessertspoon cinnamon
1 dessertspoon nutmeg
1fl oz vanilla essence
1fl oz rum
1 bottle Ruby wine
½ bottle rum
1 tablespoon caramel colour or treacle

Method
Steam all the fruit together in the Ruby wine for approximately 15 minutes, then let it cool. Cream butter and sugar together until nice and fluffy, then gradually add the eggs and caramel colour or treacle. Mix ground almonds into the flour, adding the cinnamon and nutmeg. Add the dry ingredients to the creamed butter and fold in. Finally mix all the fruit into the mixture, adding the rum flavour and vanilla essence. Place in well lined, large tin and bake for 3 hours at 325F/175C. On taking from the oven, allow to cool. Pour over the ½ bottle of rum allowing it to soak into the cake. To keep the cake nice and moist, wrap in silver foil and keep until ready for decoration.

Turkish Orange Cake

Mrs Marinos Costeletos

Ingredients

2 large unpeeled oranges
6 eggs
½lb ground almonds
½lb sugar
1 teaspoon baking powder
juice of lemon

Method
Wash and boil oranges in water for 2 hours.
Cool, cut open and remove pips. Put oranges in blender and pulp. Beat eggs and add the orange pulp and all the other ingredients, mixing thoroughly. Put into a buttered and floured cake tin, approx 10"x12". Bake in oven at 180C/350F for 50 minutes. If still wet, cook in the oven for a bit longer. Cool before turning out. Before serving, sprinkle with toasted almonds and icing sugar. Delicious served as a pudding with crème fraîche and fruit.

IV

On the Fourth day of Christmas
My true love sent to me;
Four Calling Birds,
Three French Hens,
Two Turtle Doves
and A Partridge in a Pear Tree

'Scottish Grace
Be with me, o God, at the baking of bread,
Be with me, o God, when I have fed;
Naught come to my body, my soul to pain
Naught able my contrite soul to stain.'

From the Gaelic.

Fromage à la Suisse

Serves 6

The Lady Maryel de Wichfeld

Ingredients

1½oz butter
1½oz flour
1½oz grated Parmesan cheese
½ pint milk
3 eggs (separated)
good pinch of Coleman's mustard powder
black pepper
double cream

Method
Make a thick béchamel sauce in the usual way using the butter, flour and milk. It should be very thick. Then beat in the grated Parmesan cheese and season with the black pepper. Take off the heat and allow to cool for a minute or two. Meanwhile, separate the eggs, adding the yolks to the béchamel, one at a time, and stirring well. Beat the egg whites until stiff, then stir in the mixture, a tablespoon full or two at a time to lighten the mixture, then fold in the rest of the egg whites with a fork, as you would for a soufflé.

Pour into a well buttered ring mould, and place it in a bain-marie in a hot oven for about 10 minutes, or until the top is golden brown. Remove and allow to cool. At this stage the fromage à la Suisse can be placed in the fridge to use within 24 hours, or in the deep freeze.

The next stage is to run a sharp knife around the edge of the mould and turn it onto an oven proof serving dish. Pour double cream over it abundantly and then place it in a pre-heated, hot oven. Bake in a 200C oven for about 20 minutes, or until brown crust forms on top. This is an excellent light, cheap, first course and has the great advantage that it can be made beforehand or deep-frozen.

Bacon and Spinach Salad

Serves 4-6

Mrs Theresa Pride

Ingredients

4 slices of granary bread (cubed)
8oz streaky bacon (chopped)
6oz washed young leaf spinach
4oz cheese (Feta is ideal)
1 clove garlic

Dressing
6 tablespoons wine vinegar
6 tablespoons olive oil
1 tablespoon wholegrain mustard
1 tablespoon honey
Pour into screw top jar and shake well

Method
Heat butter in large frying pan. Add garlic and cubed bread and gently fry until crisp. Remove from pan. Fry chopped bacon until crisp. Put spinach leaves, bacon and croutons into large bowl. Crumble cheese over top. Add dressing, toss and serve.

Great for lunch!

Curried Carrots

Serves 6-8

Mrs Antony Hornyold

Ingredients

12 carrots (chopped)
6 dessertspoons unsalted butter
2 dessertspoons curry powder
¼ teaspoon salt
¼ teaspoon black pepper
¼ cup fresh lemon juice
2 dessertspoons brown sugar
1 cup pecans (toasted and chopped)

Method
Having boiled chopped carrots, mix butter, curry powder, salt and pepper. Add to drained carrots. Reheat, tossing gently. Add lemon juice and sugar and toss till carrots are glazed. Sprinkle with nuts.

Mushrooms in Pastry Cases

Serves 6

Miss Ellie Constable Maxwell

Ingredients

2 large shallots
2 cloves garlic
3 tablespoons olive oil
1½oz butter
8oz chestnut button mushrooms
4oz shitake mushrooms
4oz long grain rice
3 tablespoons chopped dill
2 tablespoons crème fraîche
grated zest and juice of lemon
sea salt/black pepper

1 packet filo pastry
1½oz butter or 1 tablespoon olive oil
2 tablespoons sesame seeds

Method
Cook and drain rice.

Fry shallots and garlic in oil and place in bowl. Cut stems from shitake mushrooms and slice them. Put 1½oz of butter in pan and 3 teaspoons of oil. Fry all mushrooms over high heat for 3/4 minutes and place in bowl. Add crème fraîche, dill, lemon zest and juice, salt and pepper and mix.

Lay 2 sheets of filo pastry side by side on buttered baking sheet making a 12"x18" rectangle. Brush with butter and oil and place mushroom and rice mixture onto centre and roll up, turning corners to enclose filling. Brush with butter and sprinkle with sesame seeds. Cook in a heated oven 400F for 35-40 minutes. Serve with a green salad.

Babotie

Serves 6

Ms Angela Dunlea

Ingredients

1oz butter (plus extra for greasing)
1 tablespoon oil
1 large onion (finely chopped)
1 apple peeled (cored and chopped)
1 tablespoon curry powder
1oz white breadcrumbs
½ pint milk
2lb lean minced cooked beef
1½oz flaked almonds
3oz sultanas
juice and grated zest of 1 lemon
salt and pepper
1 egg (beaten)

Topping
2 eggs
bay leaves to garnish

Method
Preheat oven to 180C/350F/gas mark 4

Prepare ingredients. Melt butter with oil and fry the onion, apple and curry powder for 5 minutes.
Soak the bread in the milk. Mix the meat with the onion and apple. Drain breadcrumbs, press out milk and reserve. Add bread to meat. Stir in almonds, sultanas, lemon juice and zest and plenty of salt and pepper. Add the egg.
Grease a large deep dish and spoon the mixture into it. Press down to pack tightly. Next make the topping. Beat the reserved milk with the eggs, season to taste and pour over the meat mixture. Bake for about 1 hour, or until the topping has turned a bubbling golden brown. Garnish with the bay leaves.

Paella

Serves 6-8

Miss Laura Constable Maxwell

Ingredients

2½-3lb chicken (cut up with giblets)
salt and pepper
6-8 tablespoons olive oil
½lb chorizo sausages (blanched and cut in ½" slices)
1 small onion (finely chopped)
2 cloves garlic (finely chopped)
1 red or green pepper (cut into ¼" wide strips)
1¼lbs long grain rice
½lb tomatoes (peeled, de-seeded and chopped)
½ teaspoon saffron threads (dissolved in ¼ pint hot water)
½lb medium sized prawns (shelled and de-veined with tails intact)
12 or more mussels in shells (well scrubbed)
4-6oz fresh peas or asparagus tips or sliced green beans
lemon wedges to garnish

Method

Rub chicken pieces and giblets with salt and pepper. In a large, wide, flame proof casserole, brown the chicken on all sides in half of the olive oil. Remove from pan and set aside.

Add chorizo slices to pan, brown and remove. Add remaining oil to pan and sauté onion, garlic, pepper and rice for 5 minutes. Add tomatoes and cook until liquid has evaporated, stirring frequently. Blend in saffron and water. Pour in additional ¾ pint boiling water. Cook over high heat until rice has absorbed water. Pour a further ¾ pint boiling water over rice and cook until absorbed. Remove from heat, add chicken pieces and more boiling water, if needed, placing the prawns, mussels and peas on top. Place pan in a preheated 400F oven for 20 minutes. Adjust seasonings with salt and pepper and serve, garnished with lemon wedges, directly from pan.

Baby Poussin

Serves 4

Mr Esme Howard

Ingredients

2 baby poussins
fresh tarragon
salt and pepper
2 tablespoons olive oil
2-3oz butter
1 lemon
1 shallot
watercress
4 tablespoons fresh single cream
1 glass brandy

Method
Stuff each bird with one partially squeezed quarter of lemon, 1oz butter, the shallot (chopped) and a good sprig of fresh tarragon.

Flavour the cooking surfaces of the birds with the remaining lemon juice, butter and olive oil, and with salt and fresh ground pepper. (Be sure to remove any trussing).
Roast in a hot oven for 30 minutes, then pour the glass of brandy over the birds.

Cook for a further 30 minutes, or until the legs are tender. Then remove the birds from the roasting tray and carve into four portions. Add the cream to the tray and heat for several minutes stirring continually.

Cover each serving with the resulting juices, add pepper and serve garnished with fresh tarragon (off the stem) and watercress (alongside).

Delicious with new potatoes and courgettes.

Turkey (or Goose) Pilaff

Serves 4

The Hon Mrs Buchan

Ingredients

8oz cold turkey (or goose)
2oz butter
1 large onion (finely chopped)
2oz seedless raisins
1lb pork sausages (or left over forcemeat balls)
8oz Patna rice
1 pint stock or water
salt and pepper

Method
Melt butter and fry onion till soft but not brown. Add rice, stir fry for 4-5 minutes. Add stock and salt/pepper. Bring to boil, cover and cook very gently for 15 minutes. Rice should be 'al dente' and liquid gone. Add meat, raisins and remaining 1oz butter. Stir well and keep hot. Meanwhile fry sausages slowly for about 15 minutes. Put pilaff in hot dish, surround with sausages or forcemeat balls and garnish with almonds and parsley.

Chocolate Revenge

Serves 10

Mrs James Whitaker

Ingredients

1lb 4oz bitter chocolate
8 whole eggs
1lb 1oz caster sugar
12½oz unsalted butter

Method
Preheat the oven to 160C/325F/gas mark 3. Line a cake tin with greaseproof paper. Then grease and flour it.
Beat the eggs with a third of the sugar until volume quadruples. This will take at least 10 minutes in an electric mixer.
Heat the remaining sugar in a pan with 6fl oz water until the sugar has completely dissolved to a syrup.
Place the chocolate and butter in the hot syrup and stir to combine. Remove from the heat and allow to cool slightly.

Add the warm syrup to the eggs and continue to beat, rather more gently, until completely combined - about 20 seconds. Pour it into the cake tin and place in a bain-marie of hot water. It is essential, if the cake is to cook evenly, that the water comes half way up to the rim of the tin. Bake in the oven for 45 minutes. Leave to cool before serving.

Bread and Butter Pudding

Serves 4-6

Mrs Robert Hancock

Ingredients

6 brioches (sliced)
½oz candied lemon or orange peel (finely chopped)
2oz crushed almonds
½ pint milk
2½fl oz double cream
2oz caster sugar
grated rind of ½ small lemon
3 eggs
freshly grated nutmeg

Method
Pre-heat oven to gas mark 4/350F/180C.
Grease with butter a 2 pint baking dish.

Break brioches into inch size pieces. Arrange one layer over the base of the baking dish. Sprinkle the candied peel and half the crushed almonds over, then cover with another layer of the brioches and the remainder of the crushed almonds.

Next, in a glass measuring jug, measure out the milk and add the double cream. Stir in the caster sugar and lemon rind, then whisk the eggs, first on their own in a small basin and then into the milk mixture. Pour the whole lot over the brioches, sprinkle over some freshly grated nutmeg and bake in the oven for 30-40 minutes. Serve warm.

Spiced Apple Crumble

Serves 4

The Hon Mrs Buchan

Ingredients

Crumble
4oz butter
4oz fine semolina
2oz sugar
4oz flour and 1 teaspoon baking powder
1½ level teaspoons cinnamon

Apple Mix
2oz sugar
12oz apples (peeled and sliced)
very little water
3oz raisins

Method
Simmer apples and sugar with very little water till soft. Melt butter in saucepan. Stir in sugar and flour sifted with semolina and cinnamon. Press half flour mix into loose bottomed 8" sponge cake tin. Put apple purée and raisins on top. Put remaining crumble on top. Sprinkle with cinnamon. Bake in middle of oven gas mark 5 for 30 minutes. Serve hot or cold with cream. Good in freezer.

V

On the Fifth day of Christmas
My true love sent to me;
Five Gold Rings,
Four Calling Birds,
Three French Hens,
Two Turtle Doves
and A Partridge in a Pear Tree

'Without Thy sunshine and Thy rain,
We would not have Thy golden grain.
Without Thy love we'd not be fed:
We thank Thee for our daily bread.'

From the Gaelic.

Baked Eggs with Parmesan Cheese

Serves 6

Miss Vanessa de Lisle

Ingredients

2 tablespoons butter
6-8 tablespoons grated Parmesan cheese
6 eggs
½ pint thick cream
salt and pepper
6 asparagus tips (soft and tender)

Method
Butter each ramekin with 1 teaspoon of the butter, and sprinkle cheese over the bottom. Place an asparagus tip in the bottom of each ramekin. Break the egg into the dish and spoon the cream over the egg. Salt and pepper lightly. Sprinkle remaining cheese on top of egg. Dot with remaining butter and bake in a preheated oven 350F for 15 minutes.

Serve immediately.

Chicken Pie

Serves 4-6

Miss Laura Constable Maxwell

Ingredients

frozen pastry
1lb cooked chicken (diced)
salt and pepper
2 tablespoons chopped spring onions
4 teaspoons freshly grated nutmeg
3 eggs beaten
6-8 tablespoons dry white wine
½ pint cold rich chicken stock
4 hard boiled eggs (chopped)
6oz cooked artichoke hearts or asparagus tips (coarsely chopped)

Method
Roll out half the pastry and line a deep 9" pie dish. Brush with melted butter. Combine remaining ingredients, blending well and pour into the pie shell. Roll out remaining pastry and place on top, crimping edges. Make several slits in top of pastry and bake in a pre-heated oven 425F for 10 minutes. Lower heat to 325F and continue baking for 30 minutes or until golden. Serve hot or cold.

Lamb Surprise

Serves 4

Mrs John Stickney

Ingredients

1½lb sliced potatoes (old or new)
2oz melted butter
1 cooking apple (peeled, cored and sliced)
salt and pepper
8 teaspoons mint jelly
4 lamb chops

Method
Cut kitchen foil in 4 pieces each 12"x12" square and brush the centre of each with melted butter. Divide the potatoes, onion and apple evenly among the four pieces of foil. Season, and add 2 teaspoons of mint jelly onto each pile. Place a chop in each parcel, spread over remaining butter.

Seal the parcels well to prevent any meat juices escaping. Place in a baking tin and cook at 375F (gas mark 5) for 1 hour. Open and serve with a sprig of mint as garnish.

Baked Ham

Serves 6

Mr Alfred Cochrane

Ingredients

4lb joint of gammon
1 onion
1 carrot
1 stick of celery
bouquet garni
6 peppercorns

Method

Soak the joint for 4 hours in cold water to cover. Throw away the water. Cover the joint again with fresh water and bring slowly to the boil. Skim well. Add vegetables, bouquet garni and peppercorns. Cover and simmer gently for 2 hours.

Take up the joint. Remove the skin and score the fat in diamonds with a sharp knife.

Glaze
4 tablespoons golden syrup
4oz brown sugar
1 teaspoon English mustard (dry)
white wine vinegar (to moisten)
cloves
6 slices of pineapple

Place the joint in a baking tin and brush over with warmed golden syrup. Mix brown sugar and dry mustard with enough vinegar to moisten. Spread the mixture over the ham. Stick cloves on the intersecting points of the diamonds. Cover with slices of pineapple.

Bake in moderate oven 350F/gas mark 4 for 20 minutes. Serve hot with raisin sauce.

Boston Baked Beans

Serves 12

Mrs Throop Berg

Ingredients

2lbs small white pea beans
cold water to cover
4 pints cold water
boiling water
½lb well streaked salt pork
2 teaspoons salt
1 tablespoon dry mustard
2 tablespoons finely minced garlic

2 tablespoons finely minced ginger
2 bay leaves
1 teaspoon dried thyme
¼ teaspoon ground allspice
⅛ teaspoon ground cloves
1 cup dark molasses
¼ cup dark brown sugar

Method

Wash beans picking out dud ones. Cover with cold water and soak overnight. In the morning drain, put into large pan, and add 4 pints water. Bring slowly to the boiling point. Cover and simmer (do not boil) over low heat until the skins are about to burst. To test, take a few on the tip of a spoon and blow skins away.

Drain, reserving cooking liquid. Pour boiling water to cover over the salt pork and let stand for 3 minutes. Drain and cut 1" gashes into the pork without cutting into the rind, spacing the cuts about 1" apart. Put drained beans into a bean pot or casserole, add the pork and push it down until all but the rind is covered. Measure 1 cup of the bean liquid into a saucepan and stir in the mustard, salt, molasses, and brown sugar, cloves, allspice, garlic, bay leaves, ginger and thyme. Bring to boiling point and pour over the beans. Add enough of the remaining bean liquid to cover the beans, reserve any remaining liquid. Cover bean pot. Put into a very slow oven (250F). Bake for a minimum of 6-8 hours. Check for dryness about once an hour and, if necessary, add remaining bean liquid or a little boiling water, ¼ cup at a time. Beans should be moist but not soupy. Uncover the pot for the last hour to crisp the pork rind. Serve hot or cold.

Once you've eaten these you will never eat tinned baked beans again. It is a perfect accompaniment to baked ham.

Oranges with Sour Cream

Serves 8-10

Mrs Andrew Miller-Mundy

Ingredients

6 large seedless oranges
1 tablespoon brown sugar
1 cup sour cream
½ teaspoon ground cinnamon
2 tablespoons freshly grated orange peel

Method
Peel and slice oranges crosswise ¼" thick. Place on a shallow serving dish and sprinkle with brown sugar. Cover with sour cream and sprinkle with cinnamon and orange peel. Can be accompanied by meringues.

Meringues (makes 12)

Ingredients

2 egg whites
6oz caster sugar
6fl oz double cream (lightly whipped)

Method
Heat the oven to 150F/70C. Cover a baking sheet with well-greased greaseproof paper. Put the egg whites into a large bowl. Add a pinch of salt and whisk until very stiff. Whisk in half the sugar until thick, then gently fold in the remaining sugar. Spoon out onto the baking sheet and cook for at least 2½ hours until dry and crisp. Remove from the baking sheet with a palette knife and put the meringues upside down on a clean, ungreased baking tin. Return this to the oven and continue to dry them out at the lowest possible heat until all traces of sticky bottoms have vanished. The best meringues are slightly gooey inside.

Pan Forte

Serves 8-10

The Lady Julia Craig Harvey

Ingredients

3oz plain wholemeal flour
4oz plain flour
1 teaspoon ground mixed spice
½ teaspoon ground cumin
12oz clear honey
10oz crushed blanched roasted almonds
7oz mixed candied citrus peel
3oz glacé cherries
cornflower
icing sugar
cinnamon

Method
Line an 8" round sponge tin with greased greaseproof paper and preheat oven to 180C. Mix flour, spices, and add fruit and nuts, having roughly chopped the peel.

Gently heat honey in a saucepan for 10 minutes and then pour into a mixing bowl. Mix well and place it in prepared tin and pack firmly. Sprinkle mixture of cinnamon, icing sugar and cornflour and bake in centre of oven for 35 minutes. Cool on rack.

Marmalade Pudding

Serves 2 - can be doubled or trebled

Mrs Joseph Gleave

Ingredients

½ cup of self-raising flour
¼ cup of sugar
1 tablespoon of orange marmalade
¼ cup of packet suet
¼ cup of milk
¼ teaspoon bicarbonate of soda

Method
Mix dry ingredients together.
Add marmalade and bicarbonate of soda dissolved in the warm milk.
Mix paste with the dry ingredients.
Steam for at least one hour.

VI

On the Sixth day of Christmas
My true love sent to me;
Six Geese a Laying,
Five Gold Rings,
Four Calling Birds,
Three French Hens,
Two Turtle Doves
and A Partridge in a Pear Tree

'Some HA'E meat, that canna eat,
And some ha'e nane, that want it.
But we ha'e meat, and we can eat,
And sae the Lord be thankit.'

18th century. Robert Burns.

Hot Crostini

Serves 6

Mrs Marinos Costeletos

Ingredients

4oz sundried tomatoes
4 tablespoons olive oil
fresh basil
6 large slices Ciabatta
black olives

Method
Put tomatoes, basil and oil in the blender.

Toast the bread, spread with the mixture, place stoned olives and some basil leaves on top. Cut up and serve immediately.

Cheddar Cheese Soup

Serves 6

The Hon Mrs Acloque

Ingredients

1lb potatoes (peeled and diced)
½lb onions (chopped)
12fl oz water
1¼ pints beef stock
6oz cheddar cheese (grated)
4 tablespoons single cream
2-3 tablespoons butter or olive oil
2 fresh bay leaves
salt and pepper

Method
Melt the butter or oil and slowly cook (sweat) the onions and potatoes without browning in a covered pan for a few minutes.

Add the water, beef stock, bay leaves and bring to the boil. Turn down the heat and simmer until the potatoes are tender. Discard the bay leaves. Blend the vegetable mixture in a liquidizer, and add the cheese and cream and season to taste. Serve hot garnished with parsley and more cheese, if liked.

Mashed Potatoes with Celeriac and Carrots

Serves 4-6

Miss Ellie Constable Maxwell

Ingredients

celeriac
potatoes
carrots
Mozzarella cheese
milk
cream
sugar
butter

Method

Combine equal quantities of celeriac and potato to half quantity of carrots. Boil celeriac for about 20 minutes, then add the potatoes and carrots and boil until soft. Mash together, add a knob of butter, a sprinkling of sugar, a dash of milk and cream. Place in a fireproof dish. Add sliced mozzarella on top. Grill for about 30 seconds, then serve.

Pork Fillet Sauté

Serves 2

Mrs Peter Cartwright

Ingredients

2 pork fillets
4oz mushrooms
1 teaspoon paprika
2 shallots
1oz butter
3 tablespoons cream
¼ pint chicken stock
1 dessertspoon cornflour
3 tablespoons sherry

Method
Cut up fillets into bite-sized pieces, chop shallots and sauté in butter. Add paprika and cook slowly for 4 minutes. Stir in flour. Add sherry and stock. Simmer gently for 40 minutes. Sauté chopped mushrooms, add to meat. Pour on cream. Season to taste.

Roast Goose with Champ Stuffing

Serves 6-8

Mrs James Corbett

10lb goose (oven ready)
4lb potatoes (mashed)
1lb leeks (finely chopped)
2oz butter
salt and pepper

6 apples (washed and cored)
4 tablespoons sultanas and raisins
4oz brown sugar
2oz butter
6 cloves

Method
Wash the goose, remove loose fat from inside, season inside and out.
Boil and mash the potatoes.
Lightly wilt the washed leeks in the butter and add to the mashed potatoes. Season the champ.
Stuff the goose with the hot champ. Secure the opening.
Roast at gas mark 4 on a rack over a baking tray full of water for 15 minutes per lb. (The stuffing is already cooked, so need not be included in the weight calculation). Remove the goose fat as it runs into the baking tray and replace the water at intervals. Stuff the cored apples with the fruit and spice mixture. Put a dot of butter on tip of each and bake at the bottom of the oven for approx 1 hour.

When the goose is cooked (the juices from the thigh should run clear when pierced), let it rest for 10 minutes before carving. Serve with baked apple and champ.

Mushroom and Turkey Pancakes

Serves as many as required

Mrs Marc Pereire

Ingredients

Make 2 pancakes per person.

Mince leftovers from turkey.
Mince ham left overs.
Slice mushrooms and cook gently in a little oil.
Combine all ingredients.

Method
Make a white sauce, add salt and pepper. Fold the mixture into the white sauce. Put two spoonfuls on each pancake and roll the pancakes. Place pancakes in an ovenproof dish. Grate some Gruyère cheese on top. Put in a pre-heated oven for 20 minutes.

Winter Salad

Serves 6

Mrs Peter Constable Maxwell

Ingredients

2 apples (cored and diced, not peeled)
½ red cabbage (chopped)
½ white cabbage (chopped)
8oz walnuts
2 bunches watercress
2 oranges (cut into bite sized segments)

Dressing
2 cloves garlic
1 level teaspoon salt
1 teaspoon mustard powder
1½ tablespoons wine vinegar

Method
Mix all the salad ingredients together and add dressing.

Lemon Syllabub in an Almond Pastry Tart

Serves 6

Mrs Robert Hancock

Ingredients

8oz plain flour
4oz unsalted butter
2oz ground almonds
1 egg yolk
icing sugar
chilled water

Syllabub
½ pint double cream
½ pint whipping cream
grated zest of a lemon
nutmeg
cream sherry

Method
Rub flour and butter together. Then with a knife, stir in ground almonds, then the egg yolk, a tablespoon or so of sifted icing sugar and enough chilled water to bind a dough.

Chill for an hour and roll out to line a 20-25 cm tart tin. Bake blind for 25 minutes in a preheated oven at 180 C. Remove from oven and cool.

Whisk creams well. Add sherry and lemon zest, then separately whisk the egg white and fold into the cream. Dust pastry case with icing sugar and spoon in syllabub. Grate nutmeg on top before serving.

Apple and Cranberry Crumble

Serves 8

Mrs Alexander Stainow

Ingredients

1lb fresh/frozen cranberries
8 tablespoons raw sugar
4½lbs cooking apples
1 lemon squeezed
1 teaspoon allspice
1½oz butter

Crumble
4oz butter
9oz plain flour
9oz raw sugar
brown sugar
ground vanilla
ground cinnamon

Method
Set oven at 200C/400F/gas mark 6.

Choose a large oven proof dish as this recipe reduces in size whilst cooking. Put all the cranberries in the bottom and sprinkle with four tablespoons of sugar. Peel, core and slice the apples and place on the cranberries. Pour the lemon juice over the apples with the remaining sugar, sprinkle with allspice and dot with butter.

Now make the crumble. Put the butter, flour and remaining sugar in the blender and beat for up to ten seconds. Pat this mixture firmly down onto the apples and sprinkle with brown sugar and cinnamon. Bake in the oven for 35 minutes. Turn off the oven and leave there until ready to serve.

Chocolate and Vanilla Pudding

Serves 2

Mrs Jane Knight

Ingredients

4oz dark chocolate (finely chopped)
4oz butter
2 eggs
2 yolks
2oz caster sugar
approx 1½oz flour (sieved)

Method
Place butter in pan and melt, then mix in the chocolate. Add to a
mixture of 2 eggs, 2 yolks and caster sugar and beat together. Fold in
the sieved flour and pour into two greased ramekins. Steam for 8-10
minutes. Turn out and meanwhile make the sauce.

Bring 100ml milk to the boil, and then pour over a mixture of 2 egg
yolks and ½oz sugar (lightly beaten). Cover over a bain-marie,
occasionally stirring. When it thickens, add ½oz grated chocolate and
stir till melted. Pour sauce over both puddings and dust with icing
sugar.

VII

On the Seventh day of Christmas
My true love sent to me;
Seven Swans a Swimming,
Six Geese a Laying,
Five Gold Rings,
Four Calling Birds,
Three French Hens,
Two Turtle Doves
and A Partridge in a Pear Tree

'Be present at our table, Lord,
Be here and everywhere adored.
Thy creatures bless, and grant that we
May feast in Paradise with Thee'

18th century, Wesleyan grace. John Cennick.

Parsnip and Apple Soup

Serves 4-6

Mrs Robin Wickham

Ingredients

1 onion
1 clove of garlic
14oz parsnips (peeled)
½ teaspoon ground cumin
½ teaspoon ground ginger
½ teaspoon allspice
2 Bramley cooking apples
1 pint water or chicken stock
salt and freshly ground black pepper
½ pint double cream
2 tablespoons chives (finely sliced)
2 tablespoons oil

Method

Heat 2 tablespoons oil in a heavy bottomed saucepan and gently fry onions and garlic until soft, but not coloured. Add spices and continue to fry over low heat for a further minute.

Slice peeled parsnips and add to pan, cover and cook over a moderate low heat for 5 minutes, stirring regularly to prevent them from catching.

Peel, core and dice apples. Mix in with the parsnip. Cover and continue to cook for a further 5 minutes, stirring occasionally. Add the water and bring to the boil. Lower the heat, season to taste and simmer for 30 minutes or until the parsnip mixture is soft. Pour into a liquidiser, liquidise and strain.

When ready to serve, heat gently (do not boil) and add cream. Sprinkle with chives and serve with croutons or French bread.

This soup can be kept in a fridge for 24 hours.

Prawns Provençales

Serves 6

The Hon Mrs Acloque

Ingredients

1¼lbs prawns (fresh or defrosted)
2-3 medium cloves garlic (peeled)
¼lb butter
4 tablespoons fresh parsley (chopped)
6 teaspoons freshly squeezed lemon juice
6 dessertspoons dry white wine
pepper

Method
Use one clove garlic which you have sliced to rub the sides of 6 ramekins. Squeeze 1-2 more cloves garlic, depending upon your taste, and blend in a mixer, or by hand, with the butter, parsley and lemon juice.

Divide the butter mixture into 6 pats.

Divide out the prawns into the ramekins and add 1 dessertspoon of white wine to each dish and a grind of black pepper and stir.

Place a pat of butter on each dish. Place the ramekins on a baking sheet and put in a preheated oven 400F/gas mark 5 for 10 minutes or until butter has melted and prawns are hot.

Serve with crusty bread.

Smoked Mackerel Pâté

Serves 8

Mrs Theresa Pride

Ingredients

8oz smoked mackerel fillets
large tub (18oz) of Greek style natural yoghurt (or cream cheese)
chives (fresh or freeze dried)

Method
Skin and chop up the mackerel.

Stir in ¾ of yoghurt (or cream cheese) and blend to either smooth or rough consistency.

Add remaining yoghurt for creamier taste. Mix in chives.

Garnish with sprigs of parsley and serve with thinly sliced (and rolled) toast.

Mayonnaise for Fish

Serves 4

Mrs Antony Hornyold

Ingredients

4 egg yolks
¾ cup sugar
¾ cup vinegar
¾ cup cream
dessertspoon dry mustard

Method
Mix all ingredients together and cook slowly in a bain-marie until required consistency.

Hollandaise Sauce

Serves 6

Mr Richard Foster

Ingredients

6oz butter
3 eggs
small glass of white wine
dash of wine vinegar
lemon juice

Method
Whisk up yolks in food processor. Boil up one small glass of white wine, reducing down to half. Whilst whisking the egg yolks, add white wine, dash of vinegar and lemon juice.

Melt the butter in a pan, then drip it into the egg yolk mixture, whisking all the time in the processor.

Tip the combined ingredients into a bain-marie. Gradually thicken, stirring all the time and avoiding boiling.

Stuffed Rainbow Trout

Serves 4

Ms Angela Dunlea

Ingredients

4 rainbow trout (8oz each)
salt and pepper
lemon juice
butter for greasing
flat leafed parsley and lemon slices to garnish

Stuffing
2oz frozen chopped spinach
4oz Ricotta cheese
1 teaspoon flour
1 egg yolk
2 tablespoons double cream
zest and juice of ½ lemon
salt and ground black pepper
pinch of grated nutmeg

Method
Pre-heat oven to 180C/350F/gas mark 4.

Slit the fish along the belly. Remove the gut. Lay the fish, skin side up, on a board and press firmly down the backbone with the thumb. Pull out backbone and remove any bones. Season and sprinkle with lemon juice.

To make the stuffing, put the spinach into a pan and set over a low heat until the moisture has dried out. Beat in the cheese. Add the flour, egg yolk, cream, lemon zest and juice. Season with salt and pepper and add a pinch of grated nutmeg. Divide the stuffing into four and use to fill each of the boned trout, spooning it well into each cavity. Pull the fish back into shape.

Butter 4 squares of foil, slash each fish and wrap individually in foil. Place the foil parcels in a roasting tin. Pour boiling water to depth of ½" into the base of the tin and bake for 30 minutes. Serve with flat leafed parsley and lemon slices.

Tuna Carpaccio

Serves 4-5

Mrs Pat Brown

Ingredients

3oz sun-dried tomatoes in oil (drained and roughly chopped)
16 black Greek olives
2 tablespoons chopped fresh oregano
2 tablespoons minced shallots
3 tablespoons fresh lemon juice
2 tablespoons virgin olive oil
1lb fresh raw tuna
4-5 lemon wedges
8-10 slices toast

Method
Chill four or five plates.

Combine the tomatoes, olives, oregano, shallots, lemon juice and oil in a mixing bowl. Finely chop the tuna by hand.

Combine immediately before serving.

Gently mix and mound on plates. Garnish each with lemon wedge and serve with toast.

Swordfish with Soy Dijon Marinade

Serves 2

Mrs Pat Brown

Ingredients

2 swordfish steaks
1 cup soy sauce
1 tablespoon lemon zest (grated peel of lemon)
lemon juice (juice of 6 lemons)
3 teaspoons garlic (pressed)
2 tablespoons Dijon mustard
1½ cups salad oil

Method
Whisk together all marinade ingredients. Place fish in shallow pan and pour over marinade. Marinate for 2-6 hours in fridge.

Heat oil in a deep frying pan. Remember that swordfish, like tuna, is best cooked very quickly at a high temperature.

Fish Pie

Serves 4

Mrs Cherie Booth, QC

Ingredients

12oz cod
12oz smoked haddock
2 hard boiled eggs
4oz peeled prawns
3 tablespoons parsley (chopped)
1 tablespoon lemon juice
1 pint milk
1oz butter
1½oz plain flour

Topping
2lb freshly cooked potatoes
1oz butter
¼ pint warm milk

Method
Arrange fish in a baking dish and cover with milk. Bake in the oven (200C) for 15 to 20 minutes. Pour off and reserve cooking liquid for the sauce, then remove skin from fish and flake into fairly large pieces.

Melt butter in a saucepan then stir in the flour and gradually add the fish cooking liquid, stirring well until you have a smooth sauce with the thickness of double cream. Season with salt and pepper.

Mix the fish, prawns, chopped hard boiled eggs and parsley into the sauce and stir in the lemon juice. Pour into a well buttered baking dish. Cream the potatoes with the butter and warm milk and spread evenly over the fish. Bake on a high shelf for half an hour or until the top is browned.

Scallops Baked with Leeks

Serves 4

Mrs Antony Walford

Ingredients

6 medium scallops per person (24 scallops)
1 medium leek per person (4 leeks)

Béchamel sauce
10oz butter
10oz flour
1 pint milk
1 bay leaf
salt and pepper
2 cups white breadcrumbs
2oz Parmesan cheese

Method
Chop leeks and place in boiling salt water. Cook for 5-7 minutes.
Drain. Place the leeks, mixed with the béchamel sauce, into an ovenproof dish. Place scallops on top (oysters, mussels and prawns can
be used as an alternative). Sprinkle on 2 cups breadcrumbs mixed
with Parmesan cheese and place under a medium grill for 7-10
minutes until scallops are opaque.

Halve amounts to serve as an entrée.

This can also be made into a tart when placed on a short crust base
in flan tin.

Winter Fruit Salad

Serves 4

Ms Dianne Farris

Ingredients

1 packet dried mango
1 packet dried pears
1 packet dried peaches
1 lemon (cut into tiny pieces)

Method
Soak dried fruit until plumptious! Place fruit into an ovenproof serving dish. Add pieces of (unpeeled) lemon. Cover and cook in a slow oven until fruit mixture is soft and soaking in its natural juices.

Chill to serve.

Fruit Sponge

Serves 4

Ms Dianne Farris

Ingredients

1½lbs rhubarb
3oz caster sugar
juice of an orange

5oz butter
8oz caster sugar
4 large eggs (separated)
3oz dessicated coconut
4oz plain flour

Method
Butter an oven proof dish. Put rhubarb, 3oz sugar and orange juice in dish. Cover with foil and bake at gas mark 3 for 20 minutes.

Drain juice and reduce to syrup by boiling.

Cream butter and sugar together, beat in yolks and then whisk egg whites and fold in. Gradually add coconut and flour. Spread in roasting tin and put fruit and syrup on top. Put on central shelf of oven at gas mark 4/375F for about 1 hour. Cool and cut into squares.

Crème Brûlée

Serves 6

Countess Charles de Salis

Ingredients

½lb raspberries or 4 peaches (which you have peeled and sliced finely)
small packet of chopped pecans
4 egg yolks
1 pint single cream
a few drops vanilla essence
caster sugar for caramel topping

Method
Divide the fruit between 6 ramekin dishes. Sprinkle the nuts on top.

Next, in a saucepan mix egg yolks with sugar and bring to the boil. Remove from heat and add vanilla essence, stirring well. Return to heat and stir till mixture thickens. (Do not allow to boil). Cool slightly before pouring on top of fruit. Place in a cool place, preferably overnight.

Heat the grill to its hottest setting. Dust the cream with the caster sugar, which should be evenly spread. Place dishes on a flat tin and pop under the grill. The sugar should quickly melt and brown evenly. Remove from heat and allow to harden for 2-3 hours before serving.

VIII

On the Eighth day of Christmas
My true love sent to me;
Eight Maids a Milking,
Seven Swans a Swimming,
Six Geese a Laying,
Five Gold Rings,
Four Calling Birds,
Three French Hens,
Two Turtle Doves
and A Partridge in a Pear Tree

'May God bless this food to our use
and ourselves His service.
For Jesus' sake.'

Amen

Oeufs Florentines

Serves 4

Mademoiselle Marie-Lilas Schneiter

Ingredients

1 pint of béchamel sauce
1lb freshly chopped spinach
4 good sized eggs
1 tablespoon of vinegar
salt and pepper
4 tablespoons of Parmesan cheese
good quality bread (preferably wholemeal)

Method
Make a béchamel sauce, which is not too stiff. Put to one side.

Chop fresh spinach and put in rapidly boiling water. Strain off all water and set aside.

Gently simmer water with a tablespoon of vinegar in it (this helps egg to remain intact). Gently lower 4 eggs into water and poach for 3½ - 4 minutes, depending upon how you like them. Lift out with straining spoon.

Place freshly toasted buttered bread on plate. Place spinach on top, then egg and top with béchamel sauce and a sprinkling of Parmesan cheese. Place for a brief moment under grill to melt and brown cheese.

Serve immediately.

Cheese and Ham Soufflé

Serves 4

Miss Vanessa de Lisle

Ingredients

3 large eggs (separated)
3oz grated cheese (Gruyère or Parmesan)
3oz grated ham
5fl oz milk
1oz butter
1oz plain flour
cayenne pepper to taste
¼ teaspoon mustard powder
freshly grated nutmeg to taste
salt and pepper

Method
Pre-heat oven to gas mark 5/375F/190C.
Butter 1½ pint soufflé dish.

Place the milk, butter and flour in a saucepan over a medium heat and whisk until blended and thickened. Continue to cook for 3 minutes, stirring occasionally. Then add the cayenne, mustard, nutmeg, salt and pepper and leave the sauce to cool a little before stirring in the grated cheese and ham. Beat up the egg yolks, then stir them in.

Next whisk the egg whites till they are stiff, take a couple of spoonfuls and beat them into the sauce, then fold in the rest carefully. Transfer the mixture to the soufflé dish, placing it on a baking sheet in the centre of the oven and bake for 30-35 minutes. The soufflé is cooked when a skewer comes out fairly clean. Be careful not to overcook.

Cheese and Watercress Flan

Serves 6

Mrs Peter Constable Maxwell

Ingredients

8oz shortcrust pastry
1 bunch watercress
6oz cream cheese
4 eggs
a little single cream
salt and pepper
4 spring onions

Method
Line a flan case with the pastry. Wash and chop the watercress roughly. Put the eggs in a blender and gradually add the watercress until finely chopped. Put in a bowl and gradually stir in cream, cream cheese, chopped spring onion, salt and pepper. Fill the flan case and cook in the middle of a pre-heated oven 375F/gas mark 5 for 25-30 minutes until nicely browned.

Boot Pie

Serves 2

Miss Elizabeth Constable Maxwell

Ingredients

2 onions
2 bacon rashers
2 potatoes
lard
2 eggs
1oz margarine
1oz flour
½ pint milk
2-3oz cheese
cornflakes

Method
Hard boil eggs. Chop and fry the onions, then add chopped bacon and sliced potato. Add pepper and fry for 10 minutes.

Slice the eggs and put alternate layers of the mixture and egg in a greased oven proof dish.

Make a thick cheese sauce with the margarine, flour, milk and cheese. Season, pour it over the top of the pie. Sprinkle with cornflakes and cook for 40 minutes at 350F/gas mark 4.

Dolcelatte and Mascarpone Sauce

Serves 4/5

Mrs Virginia Lopalco

Ingredients

2 packs of (12oz) Pasta Reale fresh filled pasta, ravioli or tortelloni
5oz Dolcelatte cheese or any other creamy blue cheese
3oz Mascarpone or smoked cheese
700fl oz full fat milk
3 tablespoons freshly grated Parmesan
3 tablespoons fresh rosemary (finely chopped)
salt and pepper

Method
Cut the cheese into cubes and place in a saucepan with the milk. Cook gently until dissolved over a low heat. Add the fresh rosemary, cook for a couple of seconds, remove from the heat and cool slightly. Add the Mascarpone, Parmesan cheese, salt and freshly milled black pepper. Stir well until dissolved.

Cook the pasta as directed on the packet. Drain well and dress with this scrumptious sauce.

Cheese Cake

Serves 6

Ms Dianne Farris

Ingredients

approx 20 Digestive biscuits (1 packet) rolled into crumbs
¼ cup sugar
¼ cup melted butter
12oz cream cheese
½ cup sugar
¼ cup lemon juice
2 eggs (beaten)
vanilla essence
½ pint sour cream

Method
Mix the crumbs, sugar and melted butter together and place the mixture in a flan, pressing down till it is firm.

Beat the rest of the ingredients till light and fluffy. Pour onto crust and bake at 350F for 20 minutes.

Take ½ pint sour cream. Add a little sugar and 1 teaspoon vanilla essence. Whip together and spread evenly on top of cheesecake. Return to oven and cook for 10 minutes. Refrigerate for 5 hours before serving.

IX

On the Ninth day of Christmas
My true love sent to me;
Nine Ladies Dancing,
Eight Maids a Milking,
Seven Swans a Swimming,
Six Geese a Laying,
Five Gold Rings,
Four Calling Birds,
Three French Hens,
Two Turtle Doves
and A Partridge in a Pear Tree

'I am content with what I have,
Little it be or much;
And, Lord, contentment still I crave,
Because Thou savest such.'

17th century. John Bunyan

Courgette and Dill Soup

Serves 8

Dr Yana Staynov

Ingredients

2lb courgettes
1 small onion (peeled and sliced)
1 tablespoon olive oil
1½ pints chicken stock
1 heaped tablespoon cornflour
1 pint milk
½ pint single cream
1 bunch fresh dill
2oz butter
extra cream and dill for decoration

Method
Wash the courgettes, trim the ends and slice finely. Heat the oil and cook the onions gently until transparent, pour in the stock and cook for ten minutes until the courgettes are soft. Mix the cornflour with a little water and stir into the soup. Simmer for a couple of minutes then leave to cool. Liquidize the soup with the dill, milk and cream and transfer to a saucepan. Stir in the butter and simmer for a couple of minutes before serving with swirls of cream and a sprinkling of dill.

Spinach Tart

Serves 4-5

Mrs James Whitaker

Ingredients

6oz plain flour
nutmeg
pepper
salt
5oz butter
2 tablespoons water (for sprinkling)
1lb chopped cooked spinach
2 large beaten eggs
¼ pint milk
2 Spanish onions
2oz Parmesan cheese (grated)

Method
Make the pastry with the flour, 3ozs butter, pinch of salt and a sprinkling of water. Bake blind for 15 minutes in a moderate oven. Melt the remaining butter, add chopped onions and sauté until transparent. Add the spinach, milk, seasoning and eggs. Pour the mixture on the case and sprinkle with the cheese.

Bake gas mark 4/375F/180C for ½ hour.

Curried Chicken Casserole

Serves 4

Mrs Pat Brown

Ingredients

1 chicken cut into small pieces
1 onion
3 cloves garlic
3 teaspoons hot curry paste (mix with ¾ pint of water)
1 teaspoon ground ginger
6 cardamom pods
1 teaspoon coriander
1 red and 1 green pepper (sliced)
1 large tin tomatoes
salt and pepper
olive oil

Method
Cook onion, garlic and peppers in oil. Add chicken. When the chicken is slightly cooked, add herbs and curry paste mixture, salt and pepper and simmer for about 1 to 1¼ hours.

Serve with rice.

Mick's Goulash

Serves 4

Mr Michael Frith

Ingredients

2lb pork (or beef)
1 large onion
2 cloves garlic (pressed)
1 teaspoon carraway seeds
½ teaspoon paprika
1 large tin tomatoes
1 tablespoon tomato purée
salt and pepper
mixed fresh herbs (parsley, thyme or coriander)
½ pint red wine

Method
Cut pork pieces (or beef) into large chunks.

Sweat onion, garlic and carraway seed in a large frying pan. Add meat to mixture. Add paprika and tin of tomatoes. Mix in a good dollop of tomato puree and salt and pepper. Finally a mixture of fresh herbs (parsley, thyme, coriander) and red wine (plenty).

Cook slowly.

Grilled Red Mullet

Serves 4

Mrs Peter Hickman

Ingredients

4x5oz red mullet fillets.
butter
parsley (chopped)
garlic (crushed)
1 lemon
1 lime
coriander
pinch of ginger
salt and pepper

Method
Firstly create a herb paste using all of the above spices and condiments.

Scar the skin of the red mullet fillets, and fill with the herb paste. Grill under a hot grill for five minutes and serve on a spoonful of mashed potato with a green salad and large wedges of lemon.

Creamed Courgettes

Serves 6

Mrs Gregory Stainow

Ingredients

1¼lb courgettes (topped and tailed)
2 small onions (sliced into very fine rings)
2oz butter
salt and pepper
rosemary and nutmeg
¼ pint double cream

Method

Blanche the courgettes in boiling water, drain and place in cold water. Now cook the onions in the butter until soft, but not brown, preferably in a non-stick frying pan. Stir in the seasoning, rosemary and nutmeg, to taste. Add the courgettes and lastly the cream and simmer gently for five to ten minutes until the sauce is thick.

Serve with partridge or veal (either as a sauce or a vegetable).

Apricot and Hazelnut Meringue

Serves 6

Mr Nicolas Wickham Irving

Ingredients

Meringue

3 large egg whites
6oz caster sugar
3oz ground hazelnuts

Filling
4oz dried apricots (soaked before using)
juice of 1 small orange
strip of orange rind
½" cinnamon stick
1 tablespoon soft brown sugar
2 teaspoons arrowroot
½ pint double cream
toasted hazelnuts

Method
Pre-heat oven to gas mark 5/375F/190C.

Lightly oil and line with oil silicone paper two 7" sandwich tins.

Whisk egg whites till stiff, then whisk in caster sugar gradually. With a metal spoon fold in hazelnuts. Now divide the mixture equally between the two tins. Bake the meringues on the centre shelf of the oven for 20-30 minutes. Leave them in the tins to cool for 30 minutes before turning out. When cooled, loosen edges, turn on to wire racks and remove silicone strips.

With meringues in oven, start on the apricot filling. Drain the soaked apricots, then transfer them to a small saucepan and add the orange juice, rind, cinnamon and sugar, plus 2 tablespoons of the soaking water. Simmer gently for 10-15 minutes until apricots are tender, then remove the cinnamon stick and orange rind. Mix the arrowroot with a little cold water and add this to the apricot mixture, stirring over a fairly low heat, until the mixture has thickened. Then leave it to get quite cold.

To serve the meringue, whip the cream, then carefully spread the cold apricot mixture over one meringue, followed by half the whipped cream. Place the other meringue on top. Spread the remaining cream over that and decorate the top with some whole toasted hazelnuts.

Quick Almond Bavaroise

Serves 4

Mrs Marinos Costeletos

Ingredients

10 fl oz single cream
5 fl oz milk
4oz sugar
1 sachet unflavoured gelatine
4fl oz cold water
15oz sour cream
1 teaspoon almond extract

Method
Heat single cream and milk, add sugar to dissolve.

Soak gelatine in cold water, then add to hot cream mixture.

Next beat together until fluffy the sour cream and almond extract.
Stir sour cream and hot cream mixture together.

Pour into an oiled mould. Chill until set. Turn out and garnish with
fresh fruit.

Chocolate Nests

Makes 6

Children of Oxhey Nursery School, Watford

Ingredients

4oz plain chocolate (use flavoured chocolate if you prefer)
2oz sultanas
3oz cornflakes

Method
Melt chocolate in a bowl over hot water.

Stir in sultanas and cornflakes and mix well.

Spoon mixture into individual cup cakes and place in fridge for 1 hour to set.

Fudge Drops

Makes enough to treat a nursery class

Children of Oxhey Nursery School, Watford

Ingredients

5fl oz milk
1lb light brown sugar
½oz butter
½ teaspoon vanilla essence
6oz crunchy peanut butter
4oz porridge oats
4oz muesli
3oz chopped glacé cherries
salt

Method
Place the milk, sugar, and salt in a pan and bring to the boil. Stir and boil for 2 minutes until the sugar has dissolved. Take off the heat and stir in the peanut butter, oats and muesli and stir well. Spoon mixture into individual small cup cakes and leave in the fridge to set.

X

On the Tenth day of Christmas
My true love sent to me;
Ten Lords a Leaping,
Nine Ladies Dancing,
Eight Maids a Milking,
Seven Swans a Swimming,
Six Geese a Laying,
Five Gold Rings,
Four Calling Birds,
Three French Hens,
Two Turtle Doves
and A Partridge in a Pear Tree

'God! To my little meal and oil
Add but a bit of flesh to boil
And thou my pipkinnet shalt see
Give a wave-offering to thee.'

17th century. Robert Herrick

Bruges Eggs

Serves 4

The Lady Jane Ancram

Ingredients

8 eggs
1 teaspoon chopped chives
1 teaspoon chopped parsley
2oz butter
1 teaspoon French mustard
salt and pepper
¼ pint cream
8oz prawns
4oz grated cheese

Method
Hard-boil eggs, shell and chop into pieces. Place in saucepan and add the butter, cream, chives, mustard, prawns, parsley, salt and pepper. Mix well over a low heat without allowing the cream to boil. Transfer to an ovenproof serving dish, cover with the grated cheese and dot with butter. Grill under a medium grill until brown. Serve with toast.

Watercress Soup

Serves 4

Mrs Peter Constable Maxwell

Ingredients

4 bunches watercress
1 onion (peeled and chopped roughly)
2 medium potatoes (peeled and chopped)
2oz butter
1½ pints chicken stock
¼ pint double cream
salt and pepper

Method
Heat butter in a large heavy-bottomed saucepan. Cook onion till transparent. Add potatoes and chicken stock. Simmer for 20 minutes, stirring occasionally.

Add watercress, having removed the end of stalks and any wilted leaves. Heat for further 10-15 minutes. Add salt and pepper and transfer to blender. Purée according to taste - rough or smooth. Return to saucepan and heat gently, adding cream.

Dress with a sprig of watercress and serve hot or chilled.

Grilled Aubergine Pesto

Serves 4

Mrs John Berrigan Taplin

Ingredients

4 firm ripe aubergines

Pesto
6 tablespoons pine kernels
about 8oz basil leaves
6 large cloves of garlic
1½ cups good olive oil
6 tablespoons Parmesan cheese
salt and pepper

Method
Mix all the pesto ingredients in a mouli or magimix, using the
cutting blade. (By hand, a pestle and mortar is effective, but tiring).
It should end up as a rough paste, not a cream. Refrigerate until
required.

Cut each aubergine in half lengthways. Score the flesh of each half
in a criss-cross pattern. This will enable the pesto to soak in.

Bake in a moderate oven for 30 minutes. The aubergine will then be
soft to the touch. Place delicately onto a grill rack, coat each half
with a good layer of pesto, place under the pre-heated grill and after
5 minutes, when the pesto is bubbling, remove and serve.

It is imperative that this starter is eaten piping hot, before the pesto
cools. Hot bread is the perfect accompaniment.

Lamb Casserole

Serves 6

Mrs Mary Edmonds

Ingredients

12 best end neck lamb chops (you can use mutton)
¾lb button mushrooms
3 tablespoons redcurrant jelly
2 tablespoons Worcestershire sauce
3 tablespoons lemon juice
2½oz butter
2 dessertspoons flour
½ pint meat stock
¼ teaspoon nutmeg, salt and pepper

Method
Trim excess fat off chops and wash mushrooms. Heat butter in pan and brown chops quickly. Transfer to casserole, placing mushrooms on top.

In a separate saucepan slowly melt redcurrant jelly, Worcestershire sauce, lemon juice with nutmeg and seasoning.

Add flour to fat in pan. Blend in stock and mixture from saucepan. Bring to the boil, cook for 2 minutes, adjusting seasoning. Pour over chops.

Cook in a low oven for about 1¼ hours. When cooked, cool and keep in fridge over night. Next day remove fat from surface of gravy and reheat in a moderate oven.

Jugged Hare/Rabbit

Serves 4

Mr Michael Frith

Ingredients

Hare (jointed) conserve blood for marinade

Marinade
bottle red wine
finely chopped onions or shallots
garlic
sliced carrot
bay leaves
salt and pepper
fresh thyme
olive oil
fresh parsley stalks

4 rashers of bacon
½lb button mushrooms

Method
Prepare the marinade from the above ingredients and pour over jointed hare. Leave for 24 hours.

Remove hare and rub dry. Gently fry the joints in butter for 10 - 15 minutes. To seal add flour and mix in cold marinade and the removed blood and stir well.

Fry the bacon and add to hare. Top up with stock and cover meat. Tightly cover and lightly simmer for 2-3 hours.

Add mushrooms and serve with fresh chopped parsley.

Chocolate Delight

Serves 8

HRH The Duchess of Gloucester

Ingredients

6oz plain dark bitter chocolate (eg Meunier)
6oz good quality white chocolate
6 large eggs
1 teaspoon of pure vanilla essence
2 tablespoons water

Method
Break the plain chocolate into pieces and place them in a bowl over a saucepan of simmering water, not letting the water touch the bowl as it will over heat or even burn the chocolate. Repeat the same procedure with the white chocolate.

Whilst melting the chocolate, separate the eggs. Put all the egg whites in a large bowl and half of the egg yolks in one bowl and the other half in another larger bowl.

In each of the egg yolk bowls, put ½ a teaspoon of pure vanilla essence and 1 tablespoon of water and mix.

Once melted, add the dark chocolate to one bowl and the white chocolate to the other. Individually whisk each mixture (preferably using an electric whisk) until smooth and light in appearance.

Whisk the egg whites until stiff. Take a large spoonful of the whisked egg white and mix it into one of the bowls containing the chocolate/egg yolk mixture. Repeat for the second bowl.

Then carefully add half the rest of the whisked egg whites and fold each half into the two mixtures until all the egg white has been incorporated. (To do this, gently lift the bottom of the mixture to the top with a metal spoon and folding it over on itself, repeating. By doing this, you do not knock out all the air which you have beaten into the egg whites to make the mixture lighter. Also it is very important again not to overfold, as you will knock out the air you are trying to incorporate into the mousse to make it light).

Finally, add one mousse to the other, thereby creating a marbled effect and pour into your selected dish/dishes. Then allow to chill for a minimum of three hours.

Dark Banana Surprise

Serves 6

Mrs David Daukes

Ingredients

Banana Sponge

5oz butter
4½oz brown sugar (preferably soft)
4oz caster sugar
2 large beaten eggs
1 large or 2 small over-ripe mashed bananas
12¾oz plain flour
1 teaspoon baking powder
salt

Method
Cream butter and sugar together and slowly mix in eggs. Add bananas. Using a sieve, fold in flour, salt and baking powder. Cook in a greaseproof paper-lined 2lb cake tin for 55 minutes at 180C/350F/gas mark 4. Leave to cool for 15 minutes, then turn out of the tin and leave until cold.

Marbled Chocolate Custard
30fl oz custard
3oz dark chocolate (70% cocoa) melted

Gradually stir the melted chocolate into the custard, until it is partially mixed in. Pour onto the banana bread, spread gently and leave to sink in for 30 minutes.

Ganache
7fl oz double cream
2 teaspoons sugar
5oz plain chocolate
1 tablespoon butter (chopped into pieces)

Boil the cream and sugar together, mix in with the chocolate and butter. Once melted, leave to cool in the 'fridge' till set. Roll into marble sized balls and refrigerate.

Chocolate Sauce
7fl oz double cream
10oz dark chocolate
1½oz butter

Slowly melt the chocolate and cream in a bowl over hot water. Add the butter and keep warm.

Pre-heat the oven to 160C/325F/gas mark 3. Place a layer of custard soaked banana sponge onto the bases of 6 greased 8cm ramekins. Put a ball of ganache in the centre of each. Then cover with more banana sponge until the ganache is covered. Bake for 15 minutes. Serve with warm chocolate sauce.

XI

On the Eleventh day of Christmas
My true love sent to me;
Eleven Pipers Piping,
Ten Lords a Leaping,
Nine Ladies Dancing,
Eight Maids a Milking,
Seven Swans a Swimming,
Six Geese a Laying,
Five Gold Rings,
Four Calling Birds,
Three French Hens,
Two Turtle Doves
and A Partridge in a Pear Tree

'O most merciful Father, who of thy gracious goodness
hast heard the devout prayer of thy Church, and turned
our death and scarcity into cheapness and plenty; we
give thee humble thanks for this thy special bounty;
beseeching thee to continue thy loving kindness unto
us, that our land may yield us her fruits to increase thy
glory and our comfort, through Jesus Christ our Lord.

Amen'
Book of Common Prayer

Birchan Avocados

Serves 8

Mrs Robin Broke

Ingredients

4 large ripe avocados (stoned)
1 large punnet cherry tomatoes
½ pint vinaigrette (to which 2 tablespoons pesto have been added)
rocket (to garnish)

Method
Cut avocados in half. Add ½ of cherry tomatoes to vinaigrette. On each plate, place an avocado half, face up. Place 2 tablespoons of cherry tomato and vinaigrette into each hollow, allowing cherry tomatoes to spill over. Garnish with rocket leaves.

Hungarian Meatball Soup

Serves 4

Mrs Peter Newman

Ingredients

1lb lean minced beef
2oz fresh bread crumbs
1 egg (beaten)
salt and freshly ground pepper to taste
1 onion (thinly sliced)
2 tablespoons butter
1 teaspoon paprika
2 medium-size potatoes (peeled and diced)
sour cream or plain yoghurt
chopped parsley

Method
Combine the beef, bread crumbs, egg, salt and pepper. Roll into 1"
diameter balls. In a saucepan, sauté the onion in butter until
transparent, then add the paprika and 1½ pints water. Bring to the
boil, lower heat and add meatballs and potatoes. Cover and simmer
for 30 minutes. Serve in soup bowls, top each with a spoonful of
sour cream or yoghurt and sprinkle parsley on top.

Boned Chicken Stuffed with Bulgar Wheat, Apricots and Pine Nuts

Serves 4

Mrs David Daukes

Ingredients

4lb chicken (boned)
8oz bulgar wheat (hot water to soak)
3 tablespoons olive oil
4 sticks celery (finely chopped)
1 large onion (peeled and chopped)
2 cloves
4oz ready-to-eat dried apricots (chopped roughly)
2oz pine nuts
grated zest and juice of a lemon
2 tablespoons chopped fresh parsley
salt and pepper
4 rashers streaky bacon
1oz melted butter
chicken stock
1 glass dry white wine

Method

Make the stock. Prepare the stuffing by placing the bulgar wheat in a deep bowl and covering with hot water. Leave for 45 minutes, then drain.

Meanwhile fry the chopped onion, celery and garlic in the olive oil until soft. Add the pine nuts and apricots and continue to fry for a further 3-4 minutes. Now add the lemon zest, lemon juice, parsley, salt and pepper. Stir in the bulgar wheat and taste to correct seasoning.

When cool, stuff the boned bird and tie with string. Place in a roasting tin, cover the breasts with bacon rashers and then brush the whole bird with melted butter. Place the chicken in a hot oven 190C/375F and cook for 1½ hours, basting occasionally.

Boil to reduce juice and add wine and stock. Strain and serve.

Shamrock Chicken

Serves 4

Mr Stephen O'Farrell

Ingredients

4 boned breasts of chicken (diced or cut in bite-sized chunks)
2 cloves garlic
2 tablespoons honey
2 tablespoons soy sauce
2 tablespoons olive oil
2 large packets (2lb) young spinach
12oz pasta

Method
Marinate the chicken for a minimum of two hours, in the soy sauce and honey. You can add wine, if preferred.

Fry chicken in a wok with olive oil and garlic.

In a separate pan boil water and add pasta. Remove when 'al dente' and drain. While the pasta is still hot, add chicken and spinach. Stir thoroughly and serve immediately, accompanied by hot Italian bread and a good bottle of Sauvignon Blanc.

Baked Ham with Madeira and Raisin Sauce

Serves 10

Mrs Dudley Heathcote

Ingredients

4oz raisins
½ pint Madeira
1 10lb pre-cooked smoked ham

½ pint beef stock
1 onion, stuck with 2 cloves
1 bay leaf
1 teaspoon cornflower (dissolved in 1 teaspoon water)
5 orange slices (halved)
1 tablespoon butter
watercress sprigs (garnish)

Method
Soak raisins in Madeira overnight. Remove skin from ham, leaving a
¼" layer of fat. Put the ham in a roasting tin. Drain raisins, reserving
Madeira, and set aside. Add the Madeira, stock, onion and bay leaf to
the tin. Cover and bake in a pre-heated 350F oven for 1½ hours. Baste
every 20 minutes. Transfer the ham to a warm platter. Remove onion
and bay leaf from the pan and skim off as much fat as possible. Place
the tin over a high heat on top of cooker and reduce juices to a
generous ½ pint. Thicken with the cornflour. Add the reserved
raisins and simmer for 5 minutes. Stir in the butter until melted.

Slice ham and garnish with the orange slices and watercress. Pour ¼
pint sauce over the ham and serve remaining sauce on the side.

Delicious with Boston Baked Beans or baked sweet potatoes.

Mascarenhas Goan Trifle

Serves 4

Mrs Manuel Mascarenhas

Ingredients

2-3 fresh sliced mangoes (reserve some for decoration)
1 Madeira cake
1 pint of custard (or crème anglaise)
sherry (to soak cake)
4-5 passion fruit
1 pint of whipped cream

Method
Cut cake into ½" slices.
Soak in sherry and arrange in bottom of glass bowl.
Lay slices of mango over cake.
Squeeze over juice of passion fruit. Leave for 10 minutes.
Layer the custard and whipped cream on top and decorate with the mango slices.

Baked Stuffed Apples

Serves 4

Mr Lloyd W. Bowyers, Jr.

Ingredients

4 even sized cooking apples (cored)
4oz mixed dried fruits (chopped)
2 teaspoons orange rind (finely grated)
2 tablespoons raw sugar
1oz butter
4 marshmallows

Method
Pre-heat the oven to 350F/180C/gas mark 4. With the tip of a sharp knife, cut a very shallow slit in the skin around the middle of each apple. Put the apples in an ovenproof dish. Mix the dried fruits and orange rind together and fill the apples. Sprinkle each apple with a little sugar and cover with a knob of butter.

Put 4 tablespoons of water into the dish and place in the oven for 30 minutes until the apples are just soft. Pop a marshmallow on top of each apple just before the end of cooking. Alternatively, serve with whipped cream.

Pumpkin Walnut Pie

Serves 4-6

Mrs Julian Ashby.

Ingredients

Frozen shortcrust pastry

1lb pumpkin (peeled, de-seeded and chunked)
4 tablespoons double cream
2 eggs
4 tablespoons maple or golden syrup
4 tablespoons brown sugar
1 teaspoon ground cinnamon
½ teaspoon ground nutmeg
handful of shelled walnuts

Method

Cook pumpkin in a little water in a closed pan until soft - about twenty minutes. Drain pumpkin, mash and dry over the heat. Let cool, then add all remaining ingredients (except nuts) in the food processor. Process to purée.

Pre-heat oven to 400F/200C. Roll pastry on to 9" pie pan. Prick base and bake blind for 10 minutes to set pastry. Let cool a little.

Lower temperature to 325F/170C. Chop half nuts finely and sprinkle into the pastry case. Spread in filling. Decorate with remaining nut halves and bake for about an hour, until the pastry is crisp, the filling set and the top nicely browned.

XII

On the Twelvth day of Christmas
My true love sent to me;
Twelve Drummers Drumming,
Eleven Pipers Piping,
Ten Lords a Leaping,
Nine Ladies Dancing,
Eight Maids a Milking,
Seven Swans a Swimming,
Six Geese a Laying,
Five Gold Rings,
Four Calling Birds,
Three French Hens,
Two Turtle Doves
and A Partridge in a Pear Tree

'You who created, redeemed and protect us, be blessed forever. Hear our prayer, O God. We thank you, heavenly Father, for our benefactors, and humbly pray that their numbers may be increased by your generosity. Guard the Universal Church and the Christian people. Stamp out all heresy and error. Preserve our Queen and her subjects. Give us lasting peace. In the name of Christ our Lord'

Grace after meal, 16th century.
Brasenose College, Oxford

Thick Vegetable Soup

Serves 6

Mrs Peter Constable Maxwell

Ingredients

2 carrots (peeled and chopped)
3 potatoes (peeled and sliced)
1 large onion
1 tin plum tomatoes
1 leek (trimmed and sliced)
1lb spinach (washed and chopped)
3 cloves garlic
salt and pepper
butter
1 pint chicken stock

Method
Melt butter in heavy saucepan. Cook the onion over gentle heat till transparent. Add the potatoes, carrots, leeks and cook gently for 10-15 minutes. Add tin of plum tomatoes, crushed garlic, salt, pepper and chicken stock. Cook for a further ½ hour. Liquidise (consistency according to taste) and serve. Cream optional.

Lamb Braised in Beaujolais

Serves 6-8

Miss Marion Gimson

Ingredients

1 leg lamb (5-5½lb)
4 tablespoons olive oil
1 teaspoon fresh thyme
1 teaspoon fresh rosemary
1 bottle Beaujolais
8 small carrots
2 turnips
8 small red-skinned potatoes
4 small parsnips
8 shallots
3 large garlic cloves (unpeeled)
rock salt
coarse black pepper

Method

Pour 3 tablespoons olive oil in shallow roasting try and put it into the oven as it pre-heats to 350F(180C). Prepare all the vegetables, scrub the carrots, turnips and potatoes. Leave the carrots whole but chop the turnips with skins left on into quarters, and cut potatoes lengthways into 4 pieces (unpeeled). Now peel the parsnips and cut them into halves. Finally peel the shallots but leave them whole.

Remove the baking tray from the oven and place over medium heat on the hob and spoon the prepared vegetables and the unpeeled garlic into the fat. Coat the vegetables well and return to top shelf of the oven for 25-30 minutes, basting occasionally.

Meanwhile prepare lamb by placing in a roasting tin and rubbing the joint all over with the remaining olive oil and crushed rock salt and coarse black pepper.

When the vegetables are brown at the edges, remove and set aside. Place the lamb in the oven on the highest shelf and start to roast for 30 minutes.

Take the lamb out of oven and reduce the temp. to 325F(170C) and spoon off any fat to use later. Place roasting tin over medium heat on top of cooker. Pour in Beaujolais, and baste the meat with it. Then sprinkle with the chopped thyme and rosemary.

As soon as the wine begins to bubble, turn off the heat and cover the whole tin with a tent of foil (without touching the meat). Fold the foil tight under the rim of the tin and replace it in the oven, centre shelf, and continue to cook for 1½ hours.

Return to the hob, cooking gently and basting and place all the vegetables in with the lamb. Return to oven and cook for further 1½ hours.

Remove from oven and place lamb and vegetables on serving plates. Reduce the sauce over medium heat of the hob. Squeeze garlic pulp out of the skins and into the sauce and whisk in a tablespoon of redcurrant jelly. After seasoning to taste, pour sauce into warm jug and serve with lamb and vegetables.

Apostles' Casserole

(So called as it contains 12 ingredients)

Serves 20

The Reverend Malcolm McMahon

Ingredients

10 Italian Oxo cubes
2½lb pasta
2lb broccoli (broken into florets)
5oz butter
5oz flour
4 pints warm milk
1¼lb medium-strong cheddar (grated)
3lbs cooked chicken meat
2½lb sweetcorn
2 tins condensed mushroom soup
1 tin condensed cream of onion soup
1 tin condensed chicken soup

Method
Preheat oven to gas mark 5.

Cook pasta with as much water as suits you and add 5 oxo cubes. At the same time, boil broccoli in water for 3 minutes only.

Microwave chicken. The chicken should be broken into bits and skin discarded.

Melt butter, add flour and cook for 1 minute on low heat. Take pan off heat and add milk slowly, stirring to ensure blending occurs. Simmer for 2 minutes. Add broccoli, sweetcorn, condensed soup, chicken and 15oz of cheese. Stir thoroughly, until well mixed. Put into greased dishes. Top with remaining cheese. Bake 20 minutes and serve.

Turkey Upholland

Serves 4

Mrs Ann Knowles

Ingredients

4 turkey breasts
2 packets of onion soup
1 large onion
1 tomato (for slicing)
2 small cartons of single cream
1 carton measure of white wine
grated cheese

Method
Place the turkey breasts in an ovenproof dish and season well.
Add the two packets of onion soup (dry). Next, add sliced onion and
tomato, followed by the two small cartons of cream.

Fill one of the empty cartons with white wine and add to the
mixture. Scatter grated cheese on top and bake in a moderate oven
until the top is a golden brown.

Serve with fresh noodles and green salad.

Raised Pie

Serves 6

Mrs Hora den Dulk

Ingredients

12oz plain flour
5 floz water
5oz lard

A 3½lb chicken or the meat from 2-3 pheasants (uncooked)
8oz sausage meat
8oz bacon
1 tablespoon chopped fresh herbs (parsley, tarragon or thyme)
grated rind and juice of 1 orange
1 tablespoon redcurrant jelly
a pinch of freshly grated nutmeg
salt and pepper

Method
To make the pastry, melt the lard and water in a pan and bring to the boil. Put the flour in a bowl and pour over the hot liquid. Beat it all together with a wooden spoon, then press it evenly around the bottom and sides of a spring-sided tin. You won't be able to roll it out and it won't look at all nice at this stage, but don't worry, it will be all right in the end! Reserve about a quarter of the pastry for the top of the pie.

Cut up the chicken or pheasant (or a mixture of both) into chunks (not too small) and mix together in a bowl with all the other ingredients. Put this mixture into the pastry case and flatten the top. Cover the top with the remaining pastry, decorating with pastry leaves (just cut some scrap of pastry into diamond shapes). Paint with beaten egg or milk.

Cook at 200C/425F/gas mark 6 for 45 minutes. If the top is getting too brown, place a piece of greaseproof paper on top of it until the end of the cooking time. Reduce the temperature to 170C/gas mark 3 and cook for a further hour. Leave to cool before turning out. This should be served cold.

Noisettes of Lamb 'Twelve Drummers Drumming'

Serves 6

The Grenadier Guards

Ingredients

12¾oz lamb noisettes (ask your butcher to prepare these)
2oz butter
a little English mustard
6oz fresh white breadcrumbs
1 teaspoon thyme
1 teaspoon chopped parsley
a pinch of rosemary
torn fresh basil
1lb streaky bacon
12 sprues fresh green asparagus
4fl oz olive oil
3 cloves garlic (crushed)
1 teaspoon set honey
5fl oz brandy

Method
Melt the butter. Chop the parsley. Combine all herbs with the breadcrumbs and add the melted butter. Season gently with a little salt and freshly ground black pepper. Set aside.

Take the bacon and remove the rind. Wrap each noisette with a piece of bacon.

Trim the asparagus tips to about 4" lengths.
Pre- heat the oven to 200 degrees C.
Heat half of the olive oil and brown the noisettes in a frying pan. Season with a little salt and freshly ground black pepper. Remove from the pan.

Take the crushed garlic, mustard and olive oil and warm gently before brushing the mix on top of each noisette. Dip and press each noisette in the crumb mixture (to form a guardsman's bearskin!). Cook in the oven for about 10-15 minutes (the meat should be nice and pink). While the lamb is cooking, lightly cook the asparagus tips in salted boiling water for 2-3 mins, drain and keep warm.

Remove the noisettes from the pan and keep warm. Reserve the cooking juices. De-glaze the pan by flaming the brandy with the juices and the honey (and some fresh redcurrants if you can obtain them). Reduce the sauce for 1-2 mins, or until it starts to go syrupy and spoon onto the warmed plates. Place two noisettes on each plate, arrange two pieces of asparagus (to represent the drumsticks).

Leek and Potato Gratin

Serves 6

Mrs Peter Hickman

Ingredients

1lb leeks
2 onions (sliced)
1oz unsalted butter
1 pint double cream
1lb potatoes (peeled and thinly sliced)
1 small garlic clove (crushed)
salt and pepper (white)
freshly grated nutmeg
2oz Cheddar cheese (grated)

Method
Pre-heat oven to 180C/350F/gas mark 4 and grease a shallow ovenproof gratin dish. Cut the leeks diagonally into ½" slices and blanch in boiling water for 30 seconds. Drain, rinse under cold water, drain again and pat dry. Cook the onions in the butter for 2-3 minutes until softened.

In a pan, pour the cream over the sliced potatoes. Add the garlic and season with salt, pepper and nutmeg. Bring to the boil, then stir in the leeks and onions. Pour the mixture into the prepared dish to a depth of 1½", covering with all the cream. Place the dish into a roasting tray filled with very hot water and bake in the pre-heated oven for 1 hour until the potatoes are cooked through and golden brown on top. To check the potatoes during cooking, just pierce with a small vegetable knife. When it goes through easily, you will know they are cooked. Remove the dish from the hot water. As a finish, you can top with the grated Cheddar and glaze under a hot grill until golden brown.

'Instant on the Lips, Lifetime on the Hips' Cheesecake

Serves 24 in theory

The Reverend Malcolm McMahon

Ingredients

Base
1lb biscuits (ginger or chocolate digestive)
½lb butter

Filling
1lb butter
1½lb cream cheese
1½lb dark chocolate
10oz sugar
1-1½lb fresh berries (raspberries or blackcurrants)

Method
Base
Crush biscuits with a rolling pin. Melt butter and stir in biscuit crumbs until the butter is absorbed. Spoon into serving dish, greasing down firmly to form a base. Refrigerate for 2 hours until set.

Filling
Meanwhile melt butter and add to sugar. Melt chocolate (preferably in bain-marie) and add to sugar/butter mix. Add cream cheese and blend. Add fruit and blend again. Spoon filling over base. Smooth and decorate. Chill for a further 2 hours. Serve then go on a diet!

Fresh Redcurrant Flan

Serves 8

Mrs Hora den Dulk

Ingredients

Pastry
8oz plain flour
2oz caster sugar
4oz sugar
1 egg

Filling
4 tablespoons cornflour
4oz sugar
2 eggs (separated)
half pint white wine
juice and grated rind of 1 lemon
half pint double cream
1lb fresh redcurrants
3 tablespoons redcurrant jelly
2 tablespoons water

Method

First make the pastry. Put the plain flour, caster sugar, butter and egg into a food processor and process until smooth. Turn out onto a smooth surface, knead quickly and roll it out to fit a flan tin. Place in the fridge to chill for at least 30 minutes before baking blind at gas mark 5/190C for about 15 minutes, until cooked. Leave to cool.

Now make the filling. Mix the cornflour, sugar and yolks with a little wine until smooth, then add the rest of the wine and the lemon rind. Cook over a moderate heat, stirring until thick and smooth. Take off the heat and stir in the lemon juice. Whisk the egg white and fold in, then leave the mixture to cool. Whip the cream and fold into the rest of the mixture. Put the filling into the pastry case and smooth over the top.

Take the stalks off the redcurrants, wash and dry them and pile them on top of the filling, going right to the edges. Mix the redcurrant jelly and the water over a gentle heat until smooth, then brush this redcurrant glaze thickly over the redcurrants. Serve with pouring cream.

Twelve Drummers Drumming: Part Deux

A Yuletide (D)rum roll!

Serves 10

The Grenadier Guards

Ingredients

3oz flour
1oz cocoa powder
4oz caster sugar
4 eggs
1fl oz boiling water

12fl oz double cream
6oz Morello cherries
1fl oz rum
2fl oz crème de Cassis
1oz icing sugar

Method
Take the rum and crème de Cassis and gently bring to the boil.
Remove from the heat and allow to cool.

Line a baking sheet (10"x8") with lightly buttered greaseproof
paper. Place the eggs and castor sugar in a bowl and whisk over a
pan of hot water until the mixture thickens. (Be careful not to allow
the mixture to cook - it must be kept moving).
Remove from the heat and continue to whisk until the mixture is
cold. The mixture should have increased in volume by 6 fold.
Sieve the flour and cocoa powder together. Whisk in the boiling
water and then fold in the flour and cocoa with a wooden spoon.
Spread the mix evenly onto the lined tray and bake for 7-9 minutes
in a hot oven (420 deg F).

Turn out the sponge onto a clean cloth and remove the paper. Take
the liquor mixture and brush onto the sponge.
Whisk the cream until it thickens. Spread generously onto the
sponge, leaving a gap of about 1" along the length of the sponge.
Arrange the cherries on the cream (you could use raspberries if you
prefer) and carefully roll the sponge, starting from the 1" margin.
Chill and dredge in icing sugar.

Christmas Pudding

Makes 3 puddings

Mrs Robert Coles

Ingredients

1½lbs finely chopped suet (or Atora)
1lb stoned raisins
1lb currants
1lb grated carrots
1lb fresh breadcrumbs
½ teaspoon mixed spice
half nutmeg (grated)
2 eggs (well beaten)
salt
¼ pint rum
juice and grated rind of 1 lemon
3-4 tablespoons flour

Method
Mix all ingredients very well. Pack into pudding basins to within half inch of top. Cover with greaseproof paper and foil or use plastic pudding basins with plastic lids. Boil for 8 hours, filling up with boiling water as necessary.

To re-heat, boil for another 3 hours.

Make sure water is boiling before putting pudding in to cook.

Don't let it boil over the top of the basin or it will be soggy and won't keep.

After cooking, when cool, if not in plastic basin, replace greaseproof paper with a dry cloth.

Stored in cool conditions, these puddings will keep for 3 years.

Index

Vegetables

Puddings

Lemon Syllabub in a Pastry Almond Tart	80
Marmalade Pudding	70
Mascarenhas Goan Trifle	140
Old Fashioned Apple Pie	35
Oranges with Sour Cream	68
Pears in Red Wine	21
Port Jello	33
Pumpkin Walnut Pie	142
Quick Almond Bavaroise	117
Spiced Apple Crumble	59
Winter Fruit Salad	95

Cakes and Biscuits

American Brownies	22
Apricot, Prune and Walnut Mincemeat	23
Caribbean Christmas Cake	45
Chocolate Nests	118
Fudge Drops	119
Pan Forte	69
Turkish Orange Cake	46

Sauces

Hollandaise Sauce	89
Mayonnaise for Fish	88